Student Veterans and Service Members in Higher Education

D1524396

Student Veterans and Service Members in Higher Education bridges theory to practice in order to better prepare practitioners in their efforts to increase the success of veteran and military service members in higher education. Bringing together perspectives from a researcher, practitioner, and student veteran, this unique author team provides a comprehensive but manageable text reviewing relevant research literature and presenting accessible strategies for working with students. This book explores the facilitators of and barriers to student veteran learning and engagement, how culture informs the current student veteran experience, and best practices for creating and maintaining a campus that allows for the success of these students. The latest to be published in the *Key Issues on Diverse College Students* series, this volume is a valuable resource for student affairs and higher education professionals to better serve veteran and military service members in higher education.

Jan Arminio is Professor and Director of the Higher Education Program at George Mason University, USA.

Tomoko Kudo Grabosky is a licensed professional counselor and Associate Professor in the Department of Counseling Services at Shippensburg University, USA.

Josh Lang is the Co-founder of the Pennsylvania Student Veterans Coalition and business analyst at VetAdvisor® Services, USA.

KEY ISSUES ON DIVERSE COLLEGE STUDENTS

Series Editors: Marybeth Gasman and Nelson Bowman III

Asian American Students in Higher Education
Samuel D. Museus

Black Men in Higher Education: A Guide to Ensuring Student Success
J. Luke Wood & Robert T. Palmer

Student Veterans and Service Members in Higher Education
Jan Arminio, Tomoko Kudo Grabosky, & Josh Lang

Student Veterans and Service Members in Higher Education

Jan Arminio
Tomoko Kudo Grabosky
Josh Lang

Routledge
Taylor & Francis Group

NEW YORK AND LONDON

First published 2015
by Routledge
711 Third Avenue, New York, NY 10017

and by Routledge
2 Park Square, Milton Park, Abingdon, Oxon, OX14 4RN

Routledge is an imprint of the Taylor & Francis Group, an informa business

© 2015 Taylor & Francis

The right of Jan Arminio, Tomoko Kudo Grabosky, and Josh Lang to
be identified as author of this work has been asserted by him/her in
accordance with sections 77 and 78 of the Copyright, Designs and
Patents Act 1988.

Library of Congress Cataloging-in-Publication Data
Arminio, Jan L.
    Student veterans and service members in higher education/
    by Jan Arminio, Tomoko Kudo Grabosky, and Josh Lang.
    pages cm.—(Key issues on diverse college students)
    Includes bibliographical references and index.
    1. Veterans—Education (Higher)—United States. 2. Soldiers—
    Education (Higher)—United States. I. Grabosky, Tomoko Kudo.
    II. Lang, Josh. III. Title.
    UB357.A765 2015
    378.1′9826970973—dc23
    2014026982

ISBN: 978-0-415-73972-6 (hbk)
ISBN: 978-0-415-73973-3 (pbk)
ISBN: 978-1-315-81641-8 (ebk)

Typeset in Perpetua and Bell Gothic
by Florence Production Ltd, Stoodleigh, Devon, UK

Printed and bound in the United States of America by Publishers Graphics,
LLC on sustainably sourced paper.

To those who serve with fidelity for human dignity,
we dedicate this book.

Contents

Figures and Tables

FIGURES

TABLES

Series Editors' Introduction

We are pleased to introduce *Student Veterans and Service Members in Higher Education* as part of the Key Issues on Diverse College Students Series. This timely new book takes on a topic that is at the forefront of our minds—veteran students. The authors examine the student veterans' experiences and how cultural differences among veterans play a significant role in these students' transition into higher education.

Jan Arminio, Tomoko Kudo Grabosky, and Josh Lang provide the reader with not only an historical backdrop to veterans in college but also a plan for engaging current veterans on campus and ensuring that their experiences are positive and nurturing. In addition, the authors uncover the policies and practices that hinder veteran students' success on campus.

The book reveals how student veterans experience the cultures of the military and college, how cultural conflicts surface in the lives of these students, and how veteran students respond to intercultural conflicts that they face while in college.

One of a few books to tackle the subject of veteran college students, *Student Veterans and Service Members in Higher Education* lays the groundwork for future research and provides a landscape of knowledge for students and scholars alike.

Nelson Bowman III & Marybeth Gasman
Series Editors

Preface

A faculty member inquiring about how to assist student veterans and unmarried partners of deployed military service members was the genesis of this book and the research that grounds it. As a psychological counselor in higher education, Tomoko often conducted outreach to faculty, student affairs professionals, higher education administrators, and staff about obstacles to student well-being. In 2010 she reached out to Josh, an Army veteran who at the time was the president of the student veterans club at Shippensburg University, to learn more about the experience of student veterans on campus. Tomoko quickly learned about a great amount of frustration that student veterans were experiencing because they felt that the institution operated as if there were no veterans on campus. She joined with Josh and other student veterans to advocate for organizational changes to better meet the needs of student veterans. Drawing upon her expertise on cultural adjustment and cross-cultural counseling, she began sharing important information and developing resources to support student veterans' transitions from the military to campus. She became involved in supporting student veterans beyond her clinical work at the counseling center. This included supporting the student veterans' club by attending meetings, assisting in the creation and facilitation of programs and workshops, and offering support groups particular to military families as well as significant others. Josh was instrumental in planning events to honor student veterans but also in advocating on behalf of student veterans for services they needed to increase the likelihood that they would complete their degrees.

To learn more about the needs of student veterans as well as practices in higher education that support student veterans, in 2012 Tomoko created a research team that included Jan, a faculty member, Navy spouse, mother of an enlisted Navy linguist, and qualitative researcher to collect data from institutions who were known for their exemplary services for student veterans. In addition to Josh, another undergraduate veteran and graduate students from the Department of Counseling Services and the Department of Counseling and College Student

Personnel at Shippensburg University also served on the team. A grant proposal was awarded to the team by the Shippensburg University Center for Faculty Excellence in Scholarship and Teaching. The team spent two years collecting and analyzing data, and writing results. Much has happened to the three since the research and book began. Tomoko now has a son, Jan has transitioned to another institution, and Josh, now an alumnus, is working for a non-profit veteran advocacy organization he founded. Nonetheless, we all three remain committed to this important work.

WHAT THIS BOOK ADDS TO THE LITERATURE ON STUDENT VETERANS

The data collected and analyzed were sufficiently rich that Tomoko and Jan decided that writing the results in a book was more appropriate than one or several articles. There have been a number of books written about student veterans. What does this book add to the earlier texts? First, Heather Jarrow at Routledge/Taylor & Francis was supportive of the project and offered to make this book a part of their Key Issues on Diverse College Students Series edited by Marybeth Gasman and Nelson Bowman III. It is the intent of Routledge/Taylor & Francis to publish a book series based on research that offers practical insights to inform higher education practice. Each book in the series focuses on the experiences, identities, challenges, and strengths of a student group with the goal of promoting pathways to student success for all students. This goal requires providing professionals with resources on marginalized student groups. Secondly, this is a comprehensive and critical examination of the intersection of veterans and higher education. The book is comprehensive in that it moves beyond merely describing the experiences of student veteran transition. Rather, we take an in-depth exploration of the cultural ramifications of this transition for student veterans and higher education. Our discussion is critical in that we expose the unique intersections of learning, culture, equity, and politics in the lives of student veterans and higher education employees. More than a research report, this book is grounded in data and addresses the following research topics: (a) the experiences of educators, student affairs professionals, higher education administrators, and students (non-military and military) in negotiating the higher education campus; (b) facilitators of and barriers to student veteran learning and engagement; and (c) the differing practices that meet student needs and demonstrate institutional commitment. The influence of cultural differences emerged as a significant factor in student veterans' experiences in institutions of higher education and is a recurring theme of the book. The general organization is to discuss what has been published to date about the current enrollment influx of student veterans to higher education, the methodology of our study and its results, how culture informs the current student veteran experience and practice in higher education, best practices for various programs and services in higher education, and how identity and equity influence the experiences of student veterans.

STUDENT VETERANS AS A DIVERSE POPULATION

The reader might be asking, "How are student veterans considered a diverse student group?" We believe higher education has deemed some groups of students as special populations. These are students with distinctive circumstances. We do believe that student veterans deserve to be considered a special or under-represented group because they have accepted the sacrifices military service demands. They also bring experiences and an identity as a group that is unique in comparison to the general population. According to the U.S. Census Bureau (2012), less than 1% of the U.S. population is currently serving in the military and 24% of men and 2% of women in the U.S. population are veterans. The American Council on Education (ACE, 2013a) noted that more than 2 million soldiers have transitioned to civilian life after the conflicts in Iraq and Afghanistan while 5 million veterans and their families have received educational benefits. We believe too that student veterans are a special population because the public supports them receiving these distinctive educational benefits, as does the higher education community. But being prepared to serve this population is taking time. Often treated as incoming 18-year-olds, student veterans have felt isolated and unrecognized. Other students and higher education employees seemed uncertain about how to treat them. Benefits-certifying officials (if any were identified on campus) were often undertrained or overworked. College registration and payment policies did not take into consideration Veterans Administration bureaucracies and overwhelming backlogs, and military deployment and training cycles of Reservists and members of the National Guard. In the classroom student veterans were at times blamed for government decisions they had little control over or were asked how it felt to kill people. Academic and psychological counselors as well as health professionals were underprepared for aspects of war some students brought to campus with them. Basically, student veterans come from a discrete culture. Their lives are heavily influenced by sets of intersecting systems grounded in military tradition, beliefs, and assumptions. The rationale for including student veterans in this series is expressed in a lengthy quote by one of the administrator participants in our study.

They have many more experiences than first year students, and they have experiences that are unique to them . . . The veteran students that we have are a very small percentage of the population . . . For me it is addressing the needs of a group of our students. I would have done that for any group of students in need . . . It really was not out of a deep sense of patriotism or anything like that. Or out of a deep sense of trying to do the right thing for the military and so forth. Even though at one level I certainly feel all of those things. That wasn't really the motivation . . . Finding a connection with a community that supports who you are and recognizes that is an important part of how they form their identity, and how they come to understand themselves. That's why those communities are so important, and we need to mobilize the resources to help those students with that progress . . . [Student veterans] don't like the idea that at the age of 24 with their experiences and background and the kinds of things they've seen that they are now competing with 18 year olds right out of high school. They don't have a lot in common with somebody who is 17 or 18 and is worried about getting beer on the weekends. They don't connect with that experience. They also want to be able to sit down and talk to other men and women that are like minded, that want to be able to talk about what it was like to be in a position where your friends died around you, or being afraid to travel in a car because of explosive devices planted places, or to have people shoot at you, or to be alone away from your family for months, and months, and months, and months with boredom and nothing to do. To guard in the middle of night. Those kinds of experiences are things that they want to connect with and they need the support, chances are they might bump into one another, but having a veterans program that organizes those activities, we make sure that they connect with people that support them, and recognize them. It forms a sense of community, in the same way that we do with other special populations, where they have common interests and things that bind them together.

It is with this acknowledgement of Student Veterans and Service Members (SVSM) as a diverse population that we write this book.

LANGUAGE USED IN THIS BOOK

We use the term SVSM throughout the book to communicate that those with military ties on campuses are not only veterans but include those on active duty, as well as Reservists and members of the National Guard. According to the Veterans Administration (VA), veterans are men and women who have served (even for a short time), but are not currently serving, in the U.S. Army, Navy, Air Force, Marine Corps, or Coast Guard. Though technically those who served in the National Guard or Reserves are classified as veterans only if they were called up and ordered to active duty, in this text we are including those who served in the National Guard and the Reserves in our SVSM term. The VA considers veterans to be those who have been discharged under terms other than dishonorable. Those service members who have been dishonorably discharged do not have access to veteran benefits (including health care and educational benefits). Active duty military service includes full-time service in the branches named above. It also includes students attending one of the five United States Military Service Academies, but this text does not pertain to their experiences.

Other language usage that is noteworthy is our preference for the term "people of color" rather than "minority" to recognize the current demographic realities of a number of states. We also prefer the term Latino or Latina rather than Hispanic, but honor the preference of the source in cited or quoted materials.

Writing this book is contrary to the opinion of a colleague who told us, "Veterans issues are no longer issues. We're done with that." We wish that humans could find ways to settle disputes without war, but as Lair (2011) pointed out in her book on Vietnam, Congress repeatedly creates incentives that prompt the young to enlist, join, and sacrifice. Higher education colludes with these incentives, but how could educators do otherwise? As the boundaries and post-Cold-War era alliances fray, and as the VA is under scrutiny for poor and inadequate service to veterans, we regret that what educators have learned in the past 10 years in serving a substantially increased population of SVSM will most likely be needed in the near as well as distant future.

ORGANIZATION OF THE BOOK

We begin this book by offering a historical perspective of the military/higher education relationship, its collaborations and conflicts. We pay considerable attention to how veterans have had to advocate for benefits promised and how that encouraged the establishment of student veteran organizations. In Chapter 2 we present the journey we traveled to write this book. We explain the multi-site case study methodology we used in our study and describe our participants (institutions, students, and higher education employees). We provide rationale for why readers should pay attention to our findings. We move then to the influence of culture on young persons in the U.S. as they become indoctrinated into the military, then as they straddle the military and higher education, and then as they become students in U.S. higher education. Using Berry's (2005) model of assimilation, acculturation, separation, and marginalization, we offer an in-depth understanding of the student veteran experience of acculturative stress in a higher education context. This requires that we define and describe military and academic culture, their differences, how they intersect, and how students experience this intersection. We note the "mutual changes" of both dominant and subordinate groups that occur whenever such groups share the same space.

In Chapter 3 we illustrate how some well-placed dedicated educators can make an incredible difference in the lives of students and a special population. We identify what facilitates and hinders SVSM learning. We highlight the attitudes, behaviors, and leadership skills that promote the success of SVSM and perhaps any special population. What encourages and discourages a meaningful student veteran experience and from whose perspective? We offer evidence which confirms that supporting any special population requires people to advocate on behalf of individuals and groups in institutions and communities. In Chapter 4 we examine advocacy processes of student veterans and their allies. We offer a comprehensive advocacy model, a change model that can serve as a guide to higher education administrators, student affairs professionals, faculty, and staff for their own efforts. Though not attempting to deter the unique and creative ways that specific institutions serve students and address concerns, Chapter 5 provides specific best practices for institutions and a variety of services and programs in higher education. These include academic advising; assessment; career services, counseling, and disability services; enrollment management areas; residence life; campus programs and student union management; social identity resource centers that include multicultural student affairs, women's centers, and LGBT centers; student health; and veterans services.

In our study, several student veteran participants indicated they entered higher education for simply a "piece of paper." Contrarily, our findings demonstrate that significant learning occurs for even those veterans with considerable military experience. In Chapter 6 we spotlight several participants as exemplars of the learning veterans do experience in higher education. We connect these learning experiences to the literature on student development.

One of the components in the higher education context that prompts learning often different from what SVSM experienced in the military is the emphasis on equity. Examining the experiences of traditionally oppressed groups, Chapter 7 explores why the young join the military, what they experience there, and the implications for higher education as members of these groups leave a hyper-masculine environment and enter the higher education culture. We uncover equity issues in the military and wonder about the implications of those for higher education. We end the book with a bit of fortune telling. What might be the future directions and potential challenges of the work with SVSM? We explore pending legislation and ponder what has yet to be accomplished.

Considering our combined backgrounds, we represent both the military and higher education cultures. We advocate for welcoming campuses for all students and believe that campuses are evolving spaces, constructed by educators to promulgate learning potential. We pay particular attention in the book to how student veterans are a diverse population and how there are subgroups of veterans who are also members of other special populations. It is also with the acknowledgment of our desire to honor students' passions, potential, and sense of self that we seek to bridge an understanding across the military and higher education cultures.

Acknowledgments

Foremost, we acknowledge our families, friends, and colleagues and apologize that we had to sacrifice time with them to pursue this project. We must also apologize because we then asked them to read drafts and edit our work. We had considerable assistance, for which we are truly grateful, from Heather Jarrow of Routledge/Taylor & Francis as well as family members Zack Grabosky and Tom Arminio. We also would like to thank the Shippensburg University Center for Faculty Excellence in Scholarship and Teaching for funding our research project. Amber Flenner, our research assistant, helped us with data collection and an early phase of analysis. Graduate assistants at Shippensburg University including Tom Palmieri, Maria Kakavoulas, Kris Lightner, Stephanie Mcgeehan, Kate Rutland, Sara Schuch, and Devon Van Horn assisted with transcription and data analysis. Doctoral students Aoi Yamanaka and Eric Reeves at George Mason University assisted in editing and checking references. Final edits were graciously offered by Susan Jones. Marylu McEwen devoted hours reading, editing, and offering encouragement. This project would never have happened without the anonymous participants who with honesty and trust gave us their stories. We offer to all of you a hearty thousand thank-yous.

Chapter 1

Historical Context of Student Veterans and Service Members

Though most educators are at least somewhat familiar with the basic concept of the GI Bill benefits after World War II, this chapter seeks to familiarize readers with the long but inconsistent tradition of veterans benefits, how and when those benefits included education, the role of veterans themselves in advocating to receive promised benefits, how those benefits were often used for other government interests besides compensation for sacrifices made, and the evolving nature of the relationship between the military and higher education. The discussion of these historical topics provides context and precedent for this generation of SVSM and can prove useful in preventing injustices in the distribution of benefits.

A "MILESTONE" BEGINNING

Veterans were first granted benefits for serving in the Continental Army after the American Revolution. Passed in 1818, the Revolutionary War Pension Act provided benefits for both officers and the enlisted who found themselves in dire financial circumstances. These veterans had to have served at least nine months and had to swear that they were in need of assistance. According to Resch (1982),

> Historians have correctly identified this act as a milestone. It shattered nearly forty years of resistance against awarding lifetime pensions for completing military service. It created the first military pension plan and it set a precedent for later veterans programs. However, scholars have overlooked the act as the first federal effort to aid some of the nation's poor.
>
> (p. 172)

In fact, Resch concluded that this was the largest federal relief legislation until the 1900s. His research into the beneficiaries and their children indicated significant higher quality of life outcomes for those who received the benefit as compared with those veterans' children in similar circumstances whose fathers did not receive any benefits. The impact of land as a benefit was particularly beneficial to poor veterans of the American Revolution (Alexander & Thelin, 2013).

Resch (1982) noted a mix of purposes in the 1818 Act. It encouraged patriotic feelings after the War of 1812 and "assuaged guilt for earlier injustices dealt Continental soldiers" (p. 20) such as unscrupulous recruiting tactics (e.g., kidnapping and theft to pay for substitutions), moving the Army to Valley Forge, and lacking the resources to pay soldiers. According to Holt (2002), some soldiers pressured George Washington to confiscate food from filled Pennsylvania barns to feed his soldiers, but he refused. Holt also related the anecdote of soldiers at Valley Forge receiving shoes too small for their feet, so the shoes were boiled for food.

Though informal in nature, Revolutionary War military chaplains found that teaching injured soldiers to read improved their morale. Hence, chaplains held classes teaching injured soldiers to read the Bible (Persyn & Polson, 2012). Note that these efforts were not directly related to soldiers' duties.

ESTABLISHING PRECEDENT

Veterans of the War of 1812 organized "Jacksonian mass lobbying" efforts (Oberly, 1985, p. 38) to receive comparable land benefits to those Mexican War veterans received. Due to acquiring vast land from Mexico, and eagerness to populate those lands with U.S. citizens, the U.S. government granted Mexican War veterans 160 acres under the Ten Regiments Act of 1847. Veterans of the War of 1812 had received no such land grants. Though their efforts were eventually successful, massive organizing was required of various local, state, and regional veterans groups including the Veterans Corp of 1812 in New York. Holding both state and national conventions, petition drives, marches on Washington, and even advocating at funerals for equal benefits were common tactics (Oberly, 1985). These efforts coalesced veterans across social class and political divides. Veterans from the War of 1812 argued that they were worthy of these benefits because they served nobly and this was an issue of equity with other war veterans. Politicians became increasingly supportive of the veterans' demands because office holders needed votes from an electorate that was torn by issues of slavery and states' rights.

According to Oberly (1985), the U.S. government awarded 177,000 1812 veterans, widows, and their heirs land grants in 1850 and 260,000 combined War of 1812 veterans and Mexican War veterans received warrants for land. It wasn't necessarily the land that interested veterans and their families, but rather the money they could receive by selling the land to others. However, this legislation dealt only with land grants, not other types of compensation. Unfortunately, "all talk of a general pension for 1812 veterans was postponed until after the

Civil War, and by that time the veterans of the old conflict were politically overshadowed by the veterans of a new one" (Oberly, 1985, p. 55).

In 1861, a year after the Civil War began, Congress passed the First Morrill Act of 1862 which gave federal land to each senator and representative's state in Congress. Income derived from the sale of this land was to be invested in stock dividends which were to:

[c]onstitute a perpetual fund, the capital of which shall remain forever undiminished . . . and the interest of which shall be inviolably appropriated, by each State which may take claim the benefit of this act, to the endowment, support, and maintenance of at least one college where the leading object shall be, without excluding other scientific and classical studies, and including military tactics, to teach such branches of learning as related to agriculture and the mechanical arts.

(First Morrill Act, 1862, SEC. 4)

Though the money raised was far less than expected (Alexander & Thelin, 2013), curricular mandates of military training were required of all male students (Shearer, 1979), and "not universally appreciated" (Alexander & Thelin, 2013, p. 4).

Though teaching literacy in the American Revolutionary War was considered by chaplains to be a morale booster, in the Civil War such efforts by the Union Army were considered a military necessity. Enlisted soldiers who could not read and write forced officers to conduct clerical work (Shaffer, 2004). African-American soldiers realized the advantages of literacy in their post-war lives and subsequently advocated to Union leaders to establish schools (Shaffer, 2004, p. 17). According to Shaffer (2004),

Officers with abolitionist leanings also encouraged the education of black soldiers because they believed that learning would help elevate African-American soldiers. Unfortunately, the Union army formulated no general policy to make educational opportunities available to all black soldiers who desired them. Still, a number of schools for African-American troops were established through the efforts of sympathetic white officers and Northern missionaries. Most of these efforts were aimed at recently liberated slaves, but schools also appeared in regiments composed of free men of color, such as the 55th Massachusetts Infantry and the 5th Massachusetts Heavy Artillery.

(p. 17)

As research on veterans benefits from the American Revolution demonstrated, the gains to quality of life for veterans and their heirs were also significant for African American soldiers who served in the Union Army. In addition to the

3

financial benefits, other positive outcomes included training in fighting discriminatory practices in the Union Army, having some autonomy, having authority over White Southerners, and being a part of a noble cause (Shaffer, 2004). According to Shaffer (2004), Union veterans (Black and White) received three types of benefits: military claims, pensions, and access to federally funded veterans' homes, though African-American veterans at first received less pay and had to work harder to receive their benefits. Some benefits (such as signing bonuses) were retroactive and could be gained only by petitioning the federal government, a cumbersome bureaucratic process. Nonetheless, such benefits allowed African-American veterans to buy land at a significantly greater rate than African-American non veterans. Because Union Army pensions were not dependent upon the veterans' health (Costa, 1995), the cost to the government was tremendous and required significant lobbying by veterans. According to Costa, in 1862 Congress also established additional war-related disability pensions, depending upon the extent of the disability, but wealth was not a consideration. Then in 1890 Congress enacted an old-age pension for any veteran with a disability. Those veterans with a war-related disability received a higher pension. By 1910 Union veterans were collecting on average $171.90 per year. Because the Union Army pension was the only federal retirement program, receiving these pensions influenced veterans to leave the labor force before their non-veteran peers (Costa, 1995).

Another means to compensate Civil War veterans for their sacrifice was the movement to provide education for veterans' orphans. Due to the coalescing of the movements to provide public education with the concern of providing care for the deserving poor, some state governments initiated educational opportunities for Civil War orphans. Nowhere was the commitment to accommodate these children greater than in the state of Pennsylvania (Bair, 2011). In fact Pennsylvania supported such schools from 1864 until 2009. The schools were consolidated in 1893 to form the Orphans Industrial School, then renamed Scotland School for Veterans' Children in 1951 (Bair, 2011). As noted by Bair (2011), the actions of Pennsylvania demonstrated "the tension inherent in all debates about child welfare, about state responsibility of the children of deceased and disabled veterans, and about the role of education in ameliorating society's problems" (p. 463). However, the connections between education and the military were becoming much more a relationship of mutual dependency rather than purely acts of charity.

BECOMING BEDFELLOWS

The Morrill Land Grant Acts of 1862 and 1890 sought to increase the pragmatic nature of higher education. This included "the quest for sophisticated and advanced tools for warfare" (Alexander & Thelin, 2013, p. 9) and created ties between military research efforts and institutions in higher education. Whereas in the late 1890s the federal government had created and staffed its own facilities for research, it began to offer competitive research grants to research universities with sufficient resources and talent (Thelin, 2011). Studies on mustard gas, military training, the Manhattan Project, language, and cultural studies were early examples of military research conducted in conjunction with higher education. The National Science Foundation and the National Institutes of Health are "contemporary legacies" of the financial support higher education received for military-related research (Alexander & Thelin, 2013, p. 10). However, the relationship of federal government as contractor with higher education would bring tensions to the government and higher education in subsequent decades.

LESSONS OF THE BONUS MARCHERS

To quickly enhance a standing army, the Reserve Officers Training Corp (ROTC) was established in 1916 through the National Defense Act (Shearer, 1979). The first institution to offer a ROTC unit was the American Literacy, Scientific, and Military Academy in Norwich, Vermont (now Norwich University). However, ROTC students had reserved status and could not mobilize quickly. Today, ROTC programs provide a significant number of educated military officers that are "closely associated with civil society" (Alexander & Thelin, 2013, p. 6). But, in 1918, as a means to keep large numbers of active-status military personnel in college who were able to be sent to battle immediately, the Student Army Training Corps (SATC) was established within the Department of the Army as a part of the Selective Service Act of 1917 (Bower, 2004; Shearer, 1979). Shearer's (1979) case-study research investigated how the SATC was experienced at the University of Illinois, Urbana, one of the 525 institutions involved in the program (Alexander & Thelin, 2013). According to Shearer, "Every higher education institution with more than one hundred able-bodied students eighteen years old and older could participate in the program" (p. 214). This allowed institutions whose student numbers were dwindling due to the World War I draft to keep some students and, because of a 12-week on-campus training program, it provided the military inexpensive preparation for officers. The War Department footed the room, board, housing, and training costs of the SATC members. However, the War Department did not pay the full cost of tuition.

In 1918, 3,000 students were inducted into the SATC at the University of Illinois, Urbana, along with 60 military support personnel. This military presence became ubiquitous. For example, all students were told to obey military discipline, including being punctual. Confusion over academic authority and the roles of civilian versus military personnel prompted lax attendance of SATC students in civilian taught classes. Curriculum assignments were determined by War Department needs rather than faculty expectations. However, with the

Armistice signed on November 11, 1918, the SATC was disbanded, after only three months. According to Shearer, the experiment demonstrated that military leaders undervalued academic ideals and faculty resented their autonomy being undermined. Though not a success, the SATC experiment recognized the importance of a military force educated about "the most advanced technologies" (Shearer, 1979, p. 224). It also reflected the cultural conflicts between the military and higher education.

In her book describing the experiences of World War I soldiers and veterans, Keene (2001) highlighted their disgruntlement with the federal government. The draft caused soldiers to leave the labor force where their non-soldier peers were earning the highest wages in American history. The war also offered the opportunity for industrialists to make "exorbitant wartime profits" (p. 163). Unfortunately, the unemployment rate for veterans after the war was 50% higher than for their same-aged non-veteran peers. Veterans felt they "should not be unfairly punished for having done their civic duty with diminished social and economic prospects upon their return home" (p. 163). In 1924, World War I veterans were granted an adjustment to their veterans' compensation in the form of a bond in lieu of a cash payment. The bond would mature in 1945. However, during the Great Depression, veterans realized that the bond was worth little so began lobbying for an immediate cash payment. Veterans argued that this was a way to spur spending and improve the economy. As with previous veterans groups, these veterans first used the channels of letter-writing campaigns and speeches at American Legion conventions. However, in May 1932 a group of veterans struck out for Washington, DC from Portland, Oregon. Others joined and soon thousands of veterans were encamped on the Anacostia Flats, outside of Washington, DC. It is estimated that at its peak 20,000 veterans came to Washington, DC to lobby and picket lawmakers. They came to be known as the Bonus Marchers. However, President Hoover refused to meet with their leaders. In July, Hoover called on federal troops and Douglas MacArthur to force the marchers to leave by using tear gas and military armament. Veterans were distraught that their fellows in arms (current Army soldiers) would turn against them. Understanding the significant opposition to paying them the bonus by the American Legion, big business, and military leadership including Admiral Byrd (Ortiz, 2006), defeated, they returned home. At the time, the membership of the American Legion was dominated by business leaders whereas the members of the Veterans of Foreign Wars (VFW) were more working-class veterans. Consequently, the VFW was a strong supporter of the bonus. Not wanting the issue to die, the VFW instigated a media campaign (including hiring an artist and political cartoonist) to lobby for the Bonus Marchers' position (Ortiz, 2006).

Upon the election of Franklin Delano Roosevelt (FDR), the president moved quickly to pass the Economy Act of 1933 which drastically reduced federal compensation to veterans (Keene, 2001; Ortiz, 2006). This infuriated veterans who viewed FDR as a fellow veteran. Once again they felt betrayed so again they marched on Washington. Though in smaller numbers, they marched now with a more supportive general public and, due to fears of poor public relations, with a more sympathetic American Legion. FDR met with marchers and sent First Lady Eleanor to meet with them in their camp at Fort Hunt (Keene, 2001). Congress was now more supportive of the Great War veterans and by 1934 restored most of the previous veterans benefits. However, that included allowing veterans preference for jobs in the new Civilian Conservation Corp where they once again wore uniforms, were given orders, and were mandated to put a considerable amount of their pay into savings accounts (Keene, 2001). By 1936 (an election year), veterans were given their bonus and within "four months, over 98% of veterans had received full payment on their certificates" (Keene, 2001, p. 203).

The plight of the Bonus Marchers highlights the differences in social class. Their eventual ability to receive the bonus was made possible partly due to them being White men. Prior to World War II, women who served in the nurse corps were not provided any rank or benefits (Kennedy & Malone, 2009). However, granting women rank and benefits changed during World War II with the intense need for women's labor. Note too that the military was not racially integrated until 1948. The "social freedom" Black troops experienced in Europe during World War I influenced them to fight for civil rights once they returned (Keene, 2001, p. 102).

BEYOND THE WORLD WAR I BONUS: THE GI BILL

The legacy of the Bonus Marchers influenced how the next generation of veterans would be treated. This is obvious in the Servicemen's Readjustment Act of 1944, commonly known as the GI Bill, which was signed two weeks after D-Day (Keene, 2001). At the time, unemployment rates were a legitimate concern and the bill sought to alleviate economic pressure. Harry W. Colmery, a former national commander of the American Legion, is recognized as the drafter of the GI Bill (Smole & Loane, 2008). Both the House and Senate approved their own versions, which led to the bill almost failing as both chambers debated the other's versions. Fortunately, Representative John Gibson of Georgia provided a tie-breaking vote, which allowed the Senate to approve the final form of the bill on June 12 and the House on June 13 (U.S. Department of Veterans Affairs, 2013a). Benefits included mustering-out pay, unemployment insurance, educational benefits, and adequate health care (Keene, 2001). According to Keene (2001), the GI Bill was "the most comprehensive piece of social welfare legislation the United States has ever known . . . ensuring that history did not repeat itself became the primary objective both of the U.S. Army and of Great War Veterans" (p. 205). The public was generally favorable to these ideas, and the bill was considered the largest advancement of a veteran education program.

The purpose of the GI Bill was not only to offer benefits to veterans but also to keep as many veterans as possible off the unemployment lines and reentering the job market. Roosevelt's administration had already tested a work-study program that was part of the National Youth Administration (NYA) which paid students to stay in college during the post-depression era (Bower, 2004). This program "allowed college officials to select which of their students would receive aid and what type of work they would perform in return. Thus, not only would students receive the means to stay in school, but colleges would also receive a labor force" (Bower, 2004, p. 368). Students remained in school, out of the labor force, but also hopeful in the context of dire economic and geo-political conditions. In 1937 the NYA determined that verifying financial need was a requirement of the program, prompting some institutions to bow out. However, for the most part, according to Bower, this "brought New Deal-style liberalism to colleges and universities in a manner that silenced the wary and even won converts to the idea of federal involvement in postsecondary education" (p. 373).

Keene (2001) argued that the GI Bill seemed less like a bill supporting a special class (as with the World War I veteran bonus) than one program integrated into a system of social welfare programs available to deserving Americans. She asked whether these benefits "restored equality by rectifying past injustices or whether they bestowed advantages and created a specially entitled class" (p. 211). In any case, the GI Bill became a way for deserving working-class veterans to become middle class. Of course this was not possible after World War I when the average veteran had only earned a sixth grade education, whereas the average World War II veteran had earned at least two years of high school (Keene, 2001). It is not beyond reason to assume that the war had interrupted service members' educational pursuits and thus they were deserving of benefits for college. Also, to be deserving, veterans had to be honorably discharged.

The GI Bill provided $500 a year directly to a student to cover the costs of tuition, fees, books, supplies, room and board, and a living allowance, prompting veterans to pour into college campuses beginning in the fall of 1945 (Taylor, 1988). The number of veterans coming to college was double what was expected. This was a pivotal point in history at which college campuses became overwhelmed with veterans like never before. It was apparent that college campuses were unprepared to deal with the challenges of transitioning service members, which would lead to the rise of student veterans banding together on college campuses to form student veteran organizations (Student Veterans of America (SVA), 2013a). Using Arkansas State Teachers College (ASTC) as a case study, Taylor (1988) demonstrated how the institution as a whole, including its faculty and facilities, was woefully inadequate for the deluge of students, but particularly students with families. The housing shortage was acute, so too were class-rooms, other facilities, and faculty. According to Taylor, "orderly growth in the chaotic conditions" was required (p. 122). In his first-person account, Wilson offered a glimpse into this chaos.

> Registration was quite a job. The forms and blanks never seemed to apply to Tom and me, and we kept having to ask one of the clerks how to fill them out. First of all, we had to explain that we did not want to live in the college dormitories. We were told that the only students who did not have to live in dormitories were local boys who lived with their families. We said we *were* living with our families, and the clerk said that was all right, then. The next problem was filling out the form that called for the name of a "parent or guardian." At this point I was about to write down a long explanation, but Tom said a friend of his who'd been in his outfit in the Philippines and had entered Harvard under the GI Bill of Rights a term earlier had told him it would be much easier merely to list our wives as our guardians. Then the bills, official notices, and so on would automatically come to our homes, and everything would be all right. I reluctantly wrote down my wife's name. I could picture the dean having grave talks with her if I got into trouble.
>
> (Wilson, 1958, pp. 161–162)

At ASTC in 1950, veterans comprised 50% of the students and 85% of the male population. The presence of this many veterans "raised the scholarship on college campuses" (Taylor, 1988, p. 125), but some also brought with them the tragedies of war that faculty had to address with little training.

Veterans' wives often took classes or worked, but tended to be involved in campus life attending events and becoming members in campus organizations. At ASTC entrepreneurial veterans created a babysitting service and a cooperative grocery store. However, there were tensions and conflicts that came from overcrowding, county alcohol laws, and the reluctance of veterans to participate in university initiation rites.

At the University of Missouri, student veterans banded together to overcome obstacles similar to what Wilson described. Eagles and Anchors, founded on July 17, 1944, was one of the organizations formed at the University of Missouri to alleviate the transitional barriers that student veterans faced. The purpose of Eagles and Anchors was to provide aid and promote the welfare of honorably discharged veterans. The group started with only 13 veterans, but in a short period of time became known as a driving force that increased the support of veterans on campus. In the first semester they advanced their membership to 750 veterans and in the second semester to 800 of the 2,800 veterans on campus.

Eagles and Anchors advocated for a psychology course on how to study. It also co-sponsored a loan program to lower the financial burden on veterans (Mizzou Student Veterans Association, 2013).

Though the GI Bill is lauded for instigating social class mobility for millions of veterans who took advantage of it, race, gender, and religion served as barriers to its comprehensive influence. In his poignant book *Double Victory: A Multicultural History of America in World War II*, Takaki (2000) described the experiences of women, Jewish persons, and people of color in the military. As veterans they "demanded inclusion in the democracy they were defending" (p. 7). To advocate for integrating the military, in a meeting with President Truman, A. Philip Randolph, a civil rights leader said, "Negroes are in no mood to shoulder guns for democracy abroad, while they are denied democracy here at home" (p. 219). Takaki's accounts of several veterans of color who sought a better life through the GI Bill included Helen Pon Onyett who enlisted in 1942 as a nurse. She continued her service in the military for over 30 years and was promoted to the rank of full colonel in 1971. She said,

> I wouldn't have done half the things I did if I hadn't been in the service . . . I had a chance to go to school on the GI Bill . . . When I spoke before audiences, people gawked to me saying, "Oh my God, she's a colonel." Not "She's Oriental."
>
> (p. 218)

Another woman veteran noted by Takaki earned her college degree with the GI Bill and stated, "I knew what I wanted . . . and I knew that I was never gonna scrub another floor" (p. 219).

Yet, according to Turner and Bound (2003), the combination of military service and GI Benefits had "substantial positive effects on collegiate attainment" (p. 171) for White men that was not true for Black men from the South. This is because of racist state policies in the South and the lack of available institutions that would accept Black applicants. The inequality of Black schools resulted in Black veterans being less prepared for college work. Consequently, they attended trade schools in far larger numbers than colleges. Similarly, in Mississippi, of the 3,000 VA home loans issued, only two went to Black veterans (Humes, 2006). There was no Congressional oversight body to ensure the equity of access to GI Bill benefits. Filipino World War II veterans were not granted their benefits until 2009. Soon after World War II ended, the U.S. retreated from its promise of citizenship for those Filipino soldiers who fought for the U.S. (Raimundo, 2010). Though only a few examples are highlighted here, the legacy of the GI Bill should be considered in light of its realized benefits.

By 1947 veterans made up 49% of U.S. college enrollment. Across the nation, 7.8 million veterans became trained at universities, trade schools, business schools, and agriculture training programs (Reinhardt & Ganzel, 2013). As military-related research grants continued during and after World War II, so too did tensions spurred from such grants, especially in light of Senator Joseph McCarthy's hunt for academics who were disloyal to the United States. According to Thelin (2011), two questions became prominent, "Did the receipt of federal research grant funds obligate a university to submit to new tests for political compliance? And did such standards infringe on academic freedom?" (p. 275).

GROWING TENSIONS

For many research universities, the appeal of federal research dollars was too tempting to resist and the Soviet Sputnik satellite prompted an even greater emphasis from the federal government on research in the applied sciences. Hence, after World War II, the federal government surpassed private agencies in becoming a major source of funding of research institutions (Thelin, 2011). Yet, Cold War hostilities that led to the Korea and Vietnam conflicts inflamed tensions between the military and higher education.

Korea and Vietnam

There is disagreement in the literature about the havoc waged on Vietnam War veterans. Although historians such as Dean (1992) wrote that the plight of the "scorned" Vietnam veteran was largely myth, other researchers including Schwartz (1986) maintained that indeed in some ways the Vietnam veteran was worse off than other veterans. Dean's belief centers on the notion that anti-war activists used the myth of the scorned Vietnam veteran as yet another toll of the tragic conflict. He also acknowledged that how veterans fare depends on whether the veteran served prior to 1968 or later. Veteran unemployment rates did indeed rise to 11% during 1971, but decreased to 4.4% in 1973. Lastly, he argued that "veterans in the United States have become a privileged class, and that it is difficult for any politician to say 'no' to the veterans lobby" (1992, p. 69). Contrarily, Schwartz (1986) wrote that Vietnam "veterans' problems are more severe than the problems of nonveterans with similar characteristics" (1986, p. 564). Unlike veterans of previous wars, Vietnam War veterans "have not 'done as well' economically as veterans of other eras" (Schwartz, 1986, p. 564). In comparing Korean and Vietnam War veterans of similar age brackets, he found that indeed Vietnam War veterans have nearly the same mean earnings as nonveterans. He also found that the average number of years of education was a bit higher for Vietnam veterans than nonveterans, and that the pattern is the same with Korean veterans. However, both "Korean and Vietnam war veterans were more likely to have graduated from high school than nonveterans and less likely to have postgraduate training" (p. 569). According to Schwartz, Vietnam veterans were "not as able as nonveterans to translate their educational achievement into occupational achievement" (p. 69). Though a larger percentage of Vietnam War veterans took advantage of their GI benefits than Korean War veterans (72% compared to 43%), the larger availability of community college and vocational training after the Vietnam War in the 1970s than after the Korean War in the 1950s may have influenced this larger percentage.

A problem in comparing Vietnam War benefits with other era benefits is that those benefits changed several times over the course of the war. Public Law 358 was modeled after the Korean Bill of 1952 which granted stipends to veterans and service members but eliminated tuition grants to individual schools; scholarships were less than those of the Korean period (Mosch, 1971). In 1967 those benefits changed, and changed again in 1970, however limitations still existed in comparison to previous veteran benefits (Mosch, 1971). According to Mosch (1971), "[t]hese prohibitions worked against the veteran" (p. 280). The scaled-back benefits to Vietnam War veterans articulated that veterans were due only for lost time rather than as an avenue to increase class or educational mobility, which differed from the opportunities for World War II veterans (Keene, 2001). The Veterans Educational Assistance Act (VEAP) of 1976 allowed service members to make contributions that are matched on a $2 for $1 basis by the government. The benefits could be used for degree, certificate, correspondence, apprenticeship/on-the-job training programs, and vocational flight training programs. The entitlement period was from 1 to 36 months depending on the monetary contributions a service member made. Although this benefit is the oldest one still available today, approximately only 100 veterans are utilizing this benefit (U.S. Department of Veterans Affairs, 2001).

According to Boulton (2007/2008), the benefits of the Vietnam era GI Bills in 1966, 1972, and 1974 were such that attending college was a middle-class endeavor. Veterans from working-class and poor families simply could not afford to attend with what the U.S. government offered. Additional financial support was needed. Hence, college completion rates for African-American Vietnam War veterans is substantially less than for White veterans.

Regardless of the deflated educational benefits, 22 education centers were established by the Army in Vietnam, "providing evening classes for remedial education, special military training, and even college credit" (Lair, 2011, p. 124). This was not only to fight boredom and increase morale, but also to assist those service members who were "educationally deficient" (Lair, 2011, p. 124). The United States Armed Forces Institute offered correspondence courses in a range of disciplines and in trades. Also, the U.S. military contracted with the University of Maryland to provide courses at the 22 education centers.

Similar to after World War II, a group of student veterans at the University of Northern Illinois banded together to provide support for Korean War veterans (Reinhardt & Ganzel, 2013). In 1972 a group of Vietnam veterans at the

University of Wisconsin Madison formed Vets for Vets (Dean of Students Office, 2011). Both groups still exist today. As Vets for Vets was being formed, civilian students became disenchanted with large institutions and their large classrooms, impersonal bureaucracies, and seemingly pointless rules and policies. This local disenchantment of wanting a larger role in institutional governance turned to national issues. Students also wanted a voice in civil rights and ending the war in Vietnam. Likewise, "[q]uestions about the university as a home for research sponsored by the U.S. Department of Defense reached a new level of volatility in 1964 and 1965 when they became linked to growing political dissent about the United States' military presence in Southeast Asia" (Thelin, 2011, p. 309). The shootings at Kent State "propelled the campus movement into the mainstream of American news and life with a force that was wrenching and riveting" (Thelin, 2011, p. 310). According to Thelin (2011) these events caused funding agencies to withdraw grant funds for fear of disruptions.

Simultaneously, students at some institutions insisted on not allowing ROTC programs to be housed on their campuses in protest against the Vietnam War but also in protest against discrimination policies of the military. Harvard was one such institution that disbanded ROTC during the Vietnam War era and then continued the banishment because of the U.S. Defense Department's "Don't Ask Don't Tell" (DADT) policy (Field, 2004) which prevented gays and lesbians from serving openly in the military.

POST-VIETNAM ERA

In the 1960s and 1970s institutions began creating equal opportunity and non-discrimination policies and found the Defense Department was violating these discrimination policies through its ROTC programs when the military recruited on campus. Many institutions, particularly law schools, began banning military recruiters. In response, Congress passed the Solomon Act in 1994 that allowed the government to withhold Defense Department funding from institutions that disallowed military recruiters access to students (Field, 2004). In response, a coalition of law schools and other groups sued. In 2006 the case was heard by the Supreme Court, which ruled that institutions must open their campuses to military recruiters if they want access to federal funds. The repeal of DADT and the discrimination of gay and lesbian persons by the military in 2011 made the issue moot.

By 2009 there was beginning to be sincere interest in returning ROTC programs to institutions that had banned it including Columbia University (Downs, 2009). If elite institutions are to educate future national leaders, should these institutions be opposed to preparing military leaders? According to Downs (2009) in 2006 ROTC lacked 450 officers in meeting its commissioning goals and argued that educators should be concerned. He wrote, "A gulf between the military and the university is not healthy for American democracy. The constitutional order requires a civil-military relationship that protects military professionalism and autonomy, while honoring the principle and practice of civil control" (p. B8). In 2011 both Harvard and Columbia announced the re-establishment of ROTC programs at their institutions (Huckabee, 2011; Quizon, 2011).

Though President Truman signed the Women's Armed Services Act of 1948 which allowed women to serve permanently in the military (not only during a period of conflict) as long as no more than 2% of military personnel were female, women were discouraged from serving in the military during Vietnam (Kennedy & Malone, 2009). Subsequently, military educational benefits were of little significance to women at that time. This trend was reversed after Vietnam when the ceiling was lifted. The experience of women in the military is discussed in more detail in Chapter 7.

As a result of Congress ending the draft in 1972, the United States experienced military recruiting shortfalls throughout the 1980s. In response Congress has passed a number of bills offering educational benefits to spur enlistment. This is a complex list of bills with varying benefits. We describe them briefly here but also list them in Table 1.1. Note this is not a definitive description of these bills. We encourage the reader to consult the sources referenced here for more detailed information on the benefits.

Congress passed the Veteran's Educational Assistance Act of 1984, or the All-Volunteer Force Educational Assistance Program. This legislation is known today as the Chapter 30, Montgomery GI Bill. Originally, the bill provided $300 of educational assistance for 36 months if a service member completed three years of active duty or two years of active duty and four years in the Reserves. Service members were required to pay $100 of their monthly pay per month for 12 months. Reservists could also be eligible under the Chapter 1606 Selected Reserve Montgomery GI Bill for educational benefits if they are actively serving and have a six-year obligation in the Selected Reserves (U.S. Department of Veterans Affairs, n.d., p. 24).

Another benefit created during the 1980s to encourage recruitment and reenlistment was the Educational Assistance Test Act of 1981. To be eligible, service members had to enter active duty after September 30, 1980, but before October 1, 1981. The benefits are for one full academic semester or nine months for each year of active duty service, with the maximum amount of benefits being 36 months. The allowance covers educational expenses for instruction at an accredited institution. As of October 1, 2000, the total allowance for instruction may not exceed $3,524; subsistence allowance for full time training is $878, and part-time training is $439. As of August 1, 2011, break or interval pay will not be payable (U.S. Department of Veterans Affairs, 2012).

The Persian Gulf War or Operation Desert Storm proved to be a period of history when the United States provided additional benefits to military personnel and veterans. Approximately 664,000 Persian Gulf War veterans, not including Reservists, were called up for active duty, with 13.2% being women. This led Congress to pass the Persian Gulf Conflict Supplemental Authorization and Personnel Benefits Act. The legislation increased education benefits for veterans. Today, the monthly education benefit paid to veterans is based on training, length of service, and category of veteran. In addition, a veteran can participate in the "Buy-Up Program" which provides each veteran up to $5,400 if they contributed $600 while on active duty. Typically, veterans have 10 years to utilize their benefits under this program (U.S. Department of Veterans Affairs, n.d.).

Following the Montgomery GI Bill (U.S. Department of Veterans Affairs, 2013b), Congress enacted several other educational benefits. The National Call to Service program became effective October 1, 2003. This is an incentive program that requires participants to perform a period of national service. Eligible participants can choose their incentive of a $5,000 cash bonus, repayment of a qualifying student loan, not to exceed $18,000, and various monthly allowance entitlements (U.S. Department of Veterans Affairs, 2012). Another program is the Reserve Educational Assistance (REAP). Chapter 1607 is part of the Ronald Reagan National Defense Authorization Act for Fiscal Year 2005. This is a U.S. Department of Defense administered program that provides education assistance to Reservists called to active duty in response to a war or national emergency. Similar to the Montgomery GI Bill, service members have the opportunity to participate in the $600 "Buy-Up Program." The Survivors' and Dependents' Educational Assistance (DEA), previously the War Orphans' Educational Assistance Act of 1956, provides education benefits to spouses and dependents of veterans seriously injured, killed, or detained. The Marine Gunnery Sergeant John David Fry Scholarship is also available to children of individuals who, on or after September 11, 2001, gave the ultimate sacrifice while serving on active duty (Dortch, 2012).

The Post 9/11 GI Bill provides financial support for tuition, fees, and housing to veterans who served for at least 90 days of combined military service after September 10, 2001 (National Association of Independent Colleges and Universities, 2007). Currently there are approximately 923,000 veterans who are utilizing educational benefits, with 555,000 using the Post 9/11 GI Bill. The signing of the Post 9/11 GI Bill further advanced opportunities for veterans, but quickly became a challenge. The federal government did not take into account the challenges that the VA or higher education institutions would face, such as inadequate information systems and lack of staff. Consequently, veterans' benefits were not processed in a timely manner and many received improper payments (U.S. Government Accountability Office, 2011). The SVSM population grew

Table 1.1 Post-Vietnam Benefits

Program	Year Instituted	Requirement	Benefit
Survivor's and Dependents Educational Assistance (Previously War Orphans Educational Assistance Act)	1956	Spouses or dependents of service members killed, seriously injured, or detained	45 months of educational benefits toward degree, certificate, apprenticeship/ on the job training, and vocational flight training programs. Can be eligible for up to 81 months in conjunction with other VA programs.
VA Work Study Program	1972	Enrolled Veteran	Hourly wages to work with other veterans
Veterans Educational Assistance Act (VEAP)	1976	Enrolled Veterans	Service members make contributions that are matched on a $2 for $1 basis, used for degree, certificate, correspondence, apprenticeship/on the job training programs, and vocational flight training programs from 1–36 months
Educational Assistance Test Act	1981	Active duty from 9/30/1980–10/1/1981	1 semester benefit for each year of active duty, may not exceed $3,524
Veterans Assistance Act (known as Chapter 30, Montgomery GI Bill)	1984	3 years active duty	Based on number of classes taken, current monthly payment rate of $1648 multiplied by the 36-month limit
Persian Gulf Conflict Supplemental Authorization and Personnel Benefits Act	1991	Based on training, length of service, and category of veteran	10 years to use $5,400 if contribute $600

Program	Year	Eligibility	Benefits
Marine Gunnery Sergeant John David Fry Scholarship	2001	Dependents of military personnel killed on or after 9/11 while on active duty	36 months of tuition, fees, housing allowance and books and supplies stipend until age 33
National Call to Service Program	2003	National service	$5,000 cash bonus, repayment of student loan not to exceed $18,000, monthly allowance
Reserve Educational Assistance, Chapter 1607	2005	Reservists called to active duty	36 months tuition and fees based on fulltime training
Post 9/11 GI Bill	2008	Must have served 90 days after 9/10/2001	36 months of tuition and fees, housing allowance, books and supplies stipend
VetSuccess on Campus	2009	Veteran	Academic and career counseling
Veteran Opportunity to Work to Hire Heroes Act	2011	Unemployed veteran	Offers career guidance and expands education and training for 12 months

U.S. Department of Veterans Affairs. (2014a). Benefits. Retrieved from http://www.benefits.va.gov/benefits/

exponentially and many educators stepped up to support them as they made the transition while others on campus lacked the resources and understanding to provide effective support.

Due to the advocacy of many veteran service organizations to increase the support of student veterans on college campus, the VA implemented the VetSuccess on Campus program in June 2009. This program provides a full-time VA Vocational Rehabilitation and Employment Program counselor and a part-time VA outreach coordinator to assist veterans with achieving their academic and career goals. However, the VA is highly selective by choosing only institutions of higher learning with higher veteran populations (Parrish, 2013).

In 2011, Congress passed the Veteran Opportunity to Work (VOW) to Hire Heroes Act. This program is intended to support veterans who are unemployed by expanding education and training opportunities for 12 months. Under the VOW to Hire Heroes Act is the Vocational Rehabilitation program that provides education and training for veterans with a service-related disability. This benefit is also attractive to employers who are eligible for tax credits for hiring veterans (U.S. Department of Veterans Affairs, 2013d). Another popular program for the current era of veterans has been the VA work-study program. Although this program was enacted in 1972 under Public Law 92–540 it is apparent that more and more veterans are utilizing this benefit as a result of the increase of student veteran organizations on college campuses (U.S. Department of Veterans Affairs, 1990). This program gives veterans the opportunity to help alleviate some of the financial strains and the opportunity to serve their student veteran peers. In our multi-site case study, we interviewed several student veterans in this work–study program.

There are several private foundations that support the education of veterans. One is the Pat Tillman Foundation. Named in honor of Pat Tillman, a professional football player who gave up his NFL career to serve in the military after 9/11 but was later killed by friendly fire, the foundation provides annual educational scholarships for 60 military veterans and their spouses (Pat Tillman Foundation, 2014).

CURRENT STUDENT VETERAN INITIATIVES

Student Veterans of America (SVA) was founded in 2008 when student veteran organization leaders on colleges throughout the nation recognized the need to form a national coalition of student veteran organizations. In 2014, there are over 850 student veteran organizations that are members of SVA, in all 50 states and in three countries. As a coalition of student veteran groups on college campuses across the globe, SVA provides military veterans with the resources and support needed to succeed in higher education (SVA, 2013a).

Since the passage of the Post 9/11 GI Bill, non-profit organizations, the federal government, and scholars have explored innovative ways to assist veterans who transition into a college environment. Increasing the support of veterans who transition from combat to college has gained local, state, and national attention ever since September 11, 2001. Student veteran organizations throughout the country have continued to advocate for increased support of veterans on their campus.

A long-term goal of the SVA is to advocate for on-campus Veterans Resource Centers. These centers fully integrate all facets of student veteran support services, state and federal veteran programs, and student veteran organizations in one location. Furthermore, the centers usually house veteran work–study students and the veterans services coordinator or director. To address limited resources, the United States Department of Education created the Veteran Success Grant that provides a model approach to increasing the support of student veterans on a particular campus (U.S. Department of Education, 2011). In addition, the American Council on Education (ACE, 2012) offered grants to colleges to create a student veteran support program.

Despite the efforts of many student veteran organizations and college campuses to increase the support of veterans on their campus, there is still a gap in support of student veterans at the state level. For example, in Pennsylvania there are over 500 institutions of higher learning that accept VA educational approved benefits and only 43 student veteran organizations that are affiliated with SVA (SVA, 2013a). This has led several student veteran leaders, veteran service organizations, and supporters to work with state-wide officials in an effort to ease the transition to college for veterans. Some states have created legislation that mandates college campuses increase support of veterans on their campus. For example, Illinois's Higher Education Veterans Services Act provides additional requirements for schools to increase programs and services on their campuses, such as employing a veterans' services coordinator (Illinois General Assembly, 2009).

Throughout the nation, some states have developed more coordinated efforts to support student veterans. The Council of Colleges and Military Educators (CCME), a national organization, provides tools and resources to veterans and higher education professionals. Several states such as Colorado have created their own advisory councils. Operation College Promise, located in New Jersey, provides training to higher education professionals throughout the country to become certified as a veteran service provider. Another organization is the National Association of Veterans' Program Administrators that assists GI Bill certifying officials and higher education employees with a vested interest in supporting student veterans.

A recent development has been the creation of state-wide organizations that specifically support student veteran efforts. The first of its kind was the

19

Pennsylvania Student Veterans Coalition (PASVC), initiated by one of this book's authors, Josh Lang. The mission of the organization is to serve as a coalition of Student Veteran Organizations in Pennsylvania by promoting communication among organizations, advocating on their behalf, and providing resources to promote veterans' academic and career goals (PASVC, 2013). Since the creation of PASVC, Arizona, Hawaii, and Illinois have established similar organizations.

As a result of federal budget deficits, national efforts began to examine the return on investment of the Post 9/11 GI Bill, military Tuition Assistance (TA), and other forms of educational benefits for veterans. Some reports have erroneously announced a high percentage of student veterans leaving college during their first year of college (SVA, 2013b). Recently, SVA partnered with the National Student Clearinghouse and the VA to begin tracking veteran success on college campuses.

CONCLUSION

Having discussed the history of veteran benefits in the U.S., and the movements that prompted them, it may be difficult to imagine a student veteran organization advocating for educational benefits during the American Revolution. It may be easier now to view the Bonus Marchers as a precursor to today's SVA. The military, higher education, and their intersection (educational benefits for veterans) has endured a sometimes tumultuous relationship but nonetheless the relationship has endured. What can educators, student veterans, military service members, and veterans' advocates make of this history and the current context? First, there has been a relationship between an effective military and benefits for veterans almost as long as the U.S. has existed. Second, for the most part, veterans have had to advocate for their benefits and White men are more likely to take advantage of those benefits than women or soldiers of color (Gasman, 2007; Shaffer, 2004; Thelin, 2011). Also, the public view of the war in which veterans fought and the perceptions of the economic context influence veteran benefits. Consequently, these perceptions affect the educational benefits offered to veterans. Additionally, there has been a conflicting relationship between the military and higher education. The veterans' experience in higher education has been influenced by this relationship. Lastly, educational benefits for veterans not only are advantageous to individual veterans but also to their families, heirs, and society, but these benefits have not been granted equitably across groups of veterans.

Having explored the history of veterans' educational benefits and the efforts to acquire them, we begin to illustrate the SVSM experiences these benefits seek to compensate. We now examine the cultural boundaries SVSM cross to enter the military, leave the military, and enter higher education.

Chapter 2

Cultural Context

Transition studies on SVSM (Student Veterans and Military Service Members) indicate that cultural difference is one of the challenges that many SVSM experience upon entering college. For instance, Livingston, Havice, Cawthon, and Fleming (2011), in their qualitative study with 15 student veterans, found that one of the "unanticipated transitions was culture shock" (p. 326) as their participants adjusted from the highly structured and routine-based military to the less structured environment of a college campus. In another qualitative study that explored the military to college transition from the perspective of six student veteran participants, Rumann and Hamrick (2010) also noted the presence of cultural conflict in their findings. As a result of experiencing both military and academic cultures, their participants experienced role confusion and identity negotiation, which led to the development of "bi-cultural literacy" (p. 450) as they adjusted successfully to the college culture. In addition, McBain, Kim, Cook, and Snead (2012), in a recent national survey of campus programs and services for SVSM, found that despite the improvement of services and programs, one of the major issues for SVSM continues to be "social acculturation to a civilian college campus" (p. 24). These studies strongly suggest that one of the challenges of the SVSM transition is navigating the dynamics between the military culture and the culture of academia.

In this chapter, we examine cultural contexts that affect the college experience of SVSM. First, we introduce the multi-site case study we conducted to provide an in-depth look into the cultural conflict that SVSM experience in the college environment. Second, we compare and contrast the cultures of the U.S. military and U.S. higher education. Third, we describe a variety of cultural differences that SVSM experience in their transition to the college environment. Lastly, we introduce Berry's (2005) model of acculturation as a framework to organize responses of SVSM in facing the conflict between the cultures of the military and higher education.

STUDY METHODOLOGY

Before we begin our discussion on the cultural contexts of SVSM, it is imperative that we describe the nature of our study because we will incorporate our findings to illustrate the cultural conflict that SVSM in our study experienced during their transition to the military and then to higher education. Therefore, in this section, we cover the study's research team, theoretical perspective, data collection procedures, and data analysis process.

The members of our research team included the authors of this book (Arminio, Grabosky, and Lang) as well as an additional student veteran and two graduate students. Seeking to take participants and researchers to a deeper understanding of a phenomenon by uncovering aspects that have been hidden, this study utilized the theoretical perspective of interpretivism (Crotty, 1998). Furthermore, as more thoroughly discussed in Chapter 4, the Advocacy Competencies of the American Counseling Association (Lewis, Arnold, House, & Toporek, 2002) provided a lens through which to view advocacy efforts.

During the fall of 2011 and spring of 2012 we conducted a multi-site case study. A case study is "an empirical analysis that investigates a contemporary phenomenon in depth and within its real life context especially when the boundaries between phenomenon and context are not clearly evident" (Yin, 2009, p. 4). According to Merriam (2009) what makes case study as a methodology and data collection method unique "lies in delimiting the object of the study" (p. 40). This is typically referred to as its bounded system (Creswell, 2013; Merriam, 2009). We bounded our study by exploring the experiences of two multi-site institutions noted for their veteran-friendly campus initiatives. These institutions were identified by polling members of a graduate counseling and student affairs alumni Listserv and by geography. The institutions selected met our critical case, typical criterion, and purposeful sampling strategies (Creswell, 2013). Stake (2005) recommended selecting case sites that are not representative but rather sites from which researchers can most learn. This too drove our selection of one community college (CC) and one large research institution (RI) in the mid-Atlantic region. The power of a case study is not in its generalizing to other cases, but rather in its "illustrative" intent (Stake, 2005, p. 8). Talburt (2004) scolded qualitative researchers for attempting to find and prove the real, but instead stressed that the purpose of qualitative inquiry is to offer unique perspectives and new possibilities. Therefore, case studies promulgate "issue-related" studies that can "reformulate . . . assertions" (Stake, 2005, p. 10).

Both institutions had campuses that were considered by the campus community as a main campus and other outlying sites. However, both institutions were attempting to establish decentralized sites. Nonetheless, the director of campus veterans services and the campus veterans services office at both institutions were physically located at what most study participants believed to be the main campus. When researchers contacted personnel at various campuses to invite participation in our study, we were told to speak with the director at the main site. The community college was an institution with six campuses and the research institution had three campuses, with one that was divided into several locations. Researchers visited all of the campuses and locations of the research institution and two of the community college sites. In 2011 the community college had approximately 800 student veterans out of a student body of 22,000, and the research institution had 930 out of a student body of 58,000.

Data Collection Methods and Participants

Data collection methods sought to identify "ordinary happenings" (Stake, 2005, p. 29). For us data collection methods included interviews, document reviews, and observations. Interview participants included 16 higher education employees and 14 students. Twenty-one of the participants were White, three African American, one Asian American, and five Latinos. Though eight participants were women only two were student veterans (see Table 2.1). Our SVSM participants' demographics, including military and academic backgrounds, are listed in Table 2.2. Pseudonyms are used to protect the participants' identities throughout this book.

Table 2.1 Demographics of Participants (N = 30)

	Community College (n = 6)	Research University (n = 22)	Other (n = 2)
Role on Campus			
Student	2	9	1
Student Affairs Administrators	4	12	
Alumni		1	1
Race			
African American		3	
Asian American		1	
Latino/a		5	
White	6	13	2
Gender			
Female	1	5	2
Male	5	17	

Table 2.2 Demographics of SVSM Participants

Name	Social Identity	Age	Military Background	Deployment	Level	Major	Other Descriptors
Alan	White	NI	Army National Guard	Iraq 2001 & 2004	UG	Accounting	
Angelina	White	27	Army National Guard	Iraq 2005 & 2009	UG	Communication	
Ann	Asian Lesbian	25	Army National Guard	Iraq	G	Student Affairs	
Bob	White	31	Air Force	Kirgizstan, Albania, Germany, Kuwait, Qatar, Djibouti	UG	Nursing	
Carlos	Latino	40	Army & Army National Guard	Iraq 2003 & 2005	UG	Biology	
David	White	26	Army	South Korea & Iraq	G	Medicine	
Henry	White	NI	Marine Corp	Iraq 2008	UG	Undeclared	Medically retired
Jerry	White	27	Army	Germany & Iraq	U	Marketing & Political Science	PTSD
Manuel	Latino	30	Army	Iraq 2002, 2003, & 2005	U	Spanish & Urban Studies	Medically retired, PTSD
Michael	White	NI	Navy Seal	Diego Garcia, Middle East & Iraq	G	Law	
Miguel	Latino	25	Marine Corp	Pakistan, France, & Germany	UG	History & Political Science	
Steven	White	43	Army	Persian Gulf & 3 times in Iraq	U	Nursing	
Tom	White	30	Air Force Reserve	None	G	International Studies	
Tina	White	37	Spouse of Army National Guard service member	Her husband was deployed to Kuwait & Iraq	UG	Social Work	

Note. NI = no information, UG = undergraduate student, G = graduate student.

We employed semi-structured interviews allowing for participants to explore experiences that they perceived as significant to being SVSM. Yin (2009) explained that researchers have two obligations in interviewing. One is "to follow the line of inquiry determined in the case study protocol" and the other is to "ask the questions in an unbiased manner" (p. 106). The case study researcher is interested in "facts as well as opinions about events" (p. 107), hence case study interviews tend to be semi-structured and in-depth. Yin differentiated informants from respondents. Informants not only give insights about the topic being studied but also "initiate access to corroboratory or contrary sources of evidence" (p. 107). We utilized both informants and respondents. Case study interviews can also be focused, when particular information is needed. Even in the focused interview, the case study interviewer should act naïve about the topic (Yin, 2009). In semi-structured interviews researchers devise a loose interview protocol and several open-ended questions utilizing follow-up clarifying questions. Topics are worded in a way that gives participants flexibility in responding. We devised a set of pre-determined open questions but supplemented the interview with several clarifying and probing questions, such as "Can you help me understand that? Tell me more? How did that feel for you?" Examples of initial open-ended questions to student veterans included, "We would like to know about your demographic information—Could you describe yourself, in terms of age, gender, marital status, race, ethnicity, where you are from?" Subsequent interview questions of students included: "Tell us about your purpose in attending college. What was your first impression of this institution? How did you come by that impression? Tell me about your experience being a student veteran, military student, and military family member on this campus? Are there any particular incidents or experiences that stand out for you? Suppose you could create or do anything related to assisting student veterans, what would it be?" To administrators and student affairs professionals and staff we asked, "What do you think are the first impressions of this institution by student veterans or their family members? How do you think that impression is communicated? Tell me about your experiences in working with veterans and military service members, and military families on this campus. Are there any particular incidents or experiences that stand out for you? Suppose you could create or do anything related to assisting student veterans, what would it be?"

A limitation of the study was the difficulty in recruiting women participants, though four of the six research team members were women, including a student veteran. Even when we employed snowball-sampling strategies (Creswell, 2013) the number of female veteran participants was low. Therefore, we sought and interviewed women veterans outside of the two selected institutions and interviewed a female SVSM and a spouse of a male student veteran. However, this still only garnered an additional two women participants. In Chapter 7 we offer some insights about the lack of female participants.

For the study we collected documents that described the university's policies and practices related to the military student population. These documents included, but were not limited to, mission statements, policies and procedures, and materials on services from admissions, financial aid, learning center, career center, counseling center, health center, campus veterans services, and student activities. We also reviewed campus and local newspapers, magazines, newsletters, as well as blogs and Facebook pages related to student veteran issues at these two institutions. Throughout our data collection, we kept detailed records about observations, insights, and assumptions. This allowed for explicit exploration of patterns and relationships, utilizing documents to fill in gaps of stories, as well as an opportunity to confirm or challenge what we were told (Marshall & Rossman, 2011). We observed and participated in on-campus activities, meetings, and social functions. Observations occurred at public places where SVSM were likely to congregate. Glesne (2011) would describe this as being observer participants. We followed Glesne's advice that the researcher must constantly ask, "Am I making judgments rather than observations?" and "What am I seeing that I have never noticed before?" (p. 91).

Data Analysis

In following Merriam's (2009) strategies for data collection, our sense-making of the data involved "consolidating, reducing, and interpreting what people have said and what the researcher has seen and read" (p. 176). We separated written transcripts and documents into units of data that were salient to our research question, making notations next to them in the transcripts. Using a constant comparison method, these units of data and notes became codes. Out of the codes, we constructed categories. We next linked the categories and theorized about the cultural differences and other major categories that exist as SVSM transition into higher education, and how SVSM *and* institutions mutually change during this process. We discuss these interrelationships throughout this book. We begin the discussion of our findings in this chapter as we explore the cultural conflict that SVSM experience in their transition from the military to higher education.

MILITARY CULTURE

In understanding SVSM's experience, it is critical to comprehend the culture of the military that serves as the standard of conduct for the lives of military service members. Exum, Coll, and Weiss (2011) explained that "the military culture is comprised of the values, traditions, norms, and perceptions that govern how members of the armed forces think, communicate, and interact with one another and with civilians" (p. 17). Although each military branch has its unique cultural aspects, there are fundamental values that are common across all military organizations whose primary purpose is to engage in combat and to conduct war in order to defend "the homeland, national boundaries, and its citizens against aggression from neighboring adversaries or enemies" (Krueger, 2000, p. 252). To accomplish this mission, the military operates from a substantially different value system than that of civilian society. Below, we present the three aspects of the military culture that have a strong influence on the transitions of SVSM to the college environment: (a) collectivism; (b) rigid hierarchical structures; and (c) masculinity.

Collectivism

The most essential feature of the military culture is collectivism (Christian, Stivers, & Sammons, 2009). McGurk, Cotting, Britt, and Adler (2006) detailed the elements of collectivism in the military culture as follows: (a) seeing the self as part of a group; (b) placing more importance on group goals over personal goals; and (c) becoming emotionally committed to the group. Soeters (1997), in his multi-national study of value orientations in military academies, reported a significant emphasis on collectivistic values in the U.S. military. Collectivism is critical in developing a strong group identification and unit cohesiveness among military service members. Such strong cohesiveness leads to the promotion of group morale and the development of trust among unit members, which also facilitates combat-readiness (Christian et al., 2009).

Rigid Hierarchical Structures

Another defining feature of the military culture is the strong emphasis on hierarchical relationships with a clear power structure of dominance and subordination (Soeters, Poponete, & Page, 2006). For instance, the military is separated into two classes: commissioned officers (college-educated, placed in the highest leadership ranks) and enlisted (typically a college degree is not required, always under the direction of an officer). Both groups operate under a rank system that determines social status and relationships within the military. Also, the rank structure is the foundation for maintaining effective leadership and promoting a sense of responsibility and accountability among the service members to accomplish military missions. In the military, leadership and communication are established through the use of firm vertical commands, control, and reporting (Krueger, 2000).

Masculinity

Masculinity is another essential component of the U.S. military culture (Dunivin, 1994). As an institution comprised primarily of men, the military culture has been shaped by men; thus, soldiering has traditionally been viewed as a masculine role, through the notion of the combative masculine-warrior (Dunivin, 1994). A pervasive culture of male dominance still continues as men comprise 85.4% of the U.S. military's Active Duty force today (U.S. Department of Defense, 2012). There are a variety of masculine norms, values, and behaviors that are promoted in the military. For instance, self-reliance and emotional stoicism are taught to improve the chances of survival and ensure mission completion; thus, these traits are highly valued in the military (Green, Emslie, O'Neill, Hunt, & Walker, 2010). Also, masculinity plays into the military's use of power and dominance (Erhrenreich, 1997; Rueb, Erskine, & Foti, 2008) as well as the image of the ideal warrior that emphasizes violence, toughness, overt heterosexual desires, and risk-taking (Barrett, 1996: Brooks, 2001: Higate, 2007). Furthermore, the masculine model of warriors has hidden assumptions of male normalcy and female deficiency (Dunivin, 1994), and these assumptions were systemically implemented in the military in the form of the combat exclusion policy for women until the policy was finally repealed on January 23, 2013.

MILITARY CULTURE AND CIVILIAN CULTURE

Although collectivism, rigid hierarchical structures, and masculinity are essential components in military organizations, these features are significantly different from a strong and ingrained sense of individualism in U.S. society. Bedrock cultural values such as individuality, equality, personal achievement, and individual rights are the basis of U.S. civilian society; yet, these same values and behaviors violate the military ethos. Indeed, a cross-cultural study of military academies confirmed the disparities between civilian and military cultures, in that a collectivist mindset, hierarchical structures, and power differentials are more prevalent in the U.S. military than in civilian organizations (Soeters, 1997). How do American civilians become the members of a military establishment that is guided by values often in direct contrast to those of U.S. society?

The transformation of civilians into U.S. military service members begins when new military recruits experience military indoctrination, commonly known as basic training or boot camp. Throughout this intense physical and mental training, civilian individuals are trained to engage in behaviors that fall outside the norms of their civilian experience and worldviews; consequently, they are assimilated into the collective group identity of military service members (McGurk et al., 2006). Through this systematic process of military indoctrination and socialization, civilian individuals are trained to remove individualistic values and behaviors that are detrimental to military life and to view themselves as part of a collective entity (McGurk et al., 2006). In other words, new recruits are no longer American civilians as they become U.S. military service members.

HIGHER EDUCATION CULTURE

In contrast to a collectivist culture in the military, U.S. higher education is strongly rooted in ingrained individualistic values in U.S. culture, as the structure and functioning of the educational system is mediated by the underlying culture of the society (Hofstede, 2001). Indeed, describing the U.S. classroom culture to international students, Smithee, Greenblatt, and Eland (2004) explained that U.S. classroom environments are based on individualistic values, personal responsibility, independent thinking, and democratic principles.

The cultural dimension of individualism–collectivism has been studied extensively to understand a variety of cultural differences including education-related issues. Research suggests that students' individualist–collectivist value perspectives will present quite different interests, values, and interpretations and corresponding behaviors to a specific learning context (Frankel, Swanson, & Sagan, 2005). For example, an institution's collectivism–individualism orientation influences students' educational goals, distribution of resources, preference of academic activities, patterns of discourse and communication, and ways to deal with conflict (Frankel et al., 2005). However, most of the research about the individualism–collectivism dimension on educational issues has focused on students from different countries or ethnic and racial backgrounds. Therefore, little is known about how the individualism–collectivism dimension influences the SVSM experience in the educational context of U.S. higher education.

Given the substantial differences that exist between the military and the context of U.S. higher education, how do SVSM experience this cultural shift in their transition from the military to college? In the next section, we detail our research findings that describe the cultural transition that SVSM encountered as college students.

CULTURAL DIFFERENCES

Many SVSM participants in our study described their transition to college as navigating cultural dissonance between the military and college life. This cultural dissonance was experienced mainly through the loss of a military culture that is preserved through collectivism, rigid structures, and masculinity. Simultaneously, our SVSM participants identified the distinct culture of academia that emphasizes individualism, freedom of choice, interactive learning, independent thinking, and equal relationships. These immense cultural differences complicate the transition process to higher education. Below, we describe how cultural conflict surfaced in the lives of our SVSM participants.

Loss of Structures

The most challenging difference for many of our SVSM participants was the loss of clear structures and detailed directions that the military provided to govern service members' lives. This finding is consistent with other SVSM transition studies' results (Livingston et al., 2011: Rumann & Hamrick, 2010). Like participants in other studies, once on campus, our SVSM participants realized that their lives were no longer as clearly structured by external forces as they had been in the military. Manuel lamented:

> [My transition] was rough because I was used to having structures and certain routines every day, even over the weekends . . . It took a while to get used to dealing with things on my own and not having someone telling me what to do or set rules to abide by.

As seen in Manuel's statements, many of our SVSM participants felt lost without authoritative direction as they began their lives in the culture of academia that values individual freedom and respect for autonomy. In college, students are expected to be responsible for developing their own structures and directions in their lives. Yet, this task was unfamiliar for many SVSM. Carlos stated:

> [In college] there's no command structure, and you have freedom. I think one of the biggest challenges is . . . you're coming out of an environment that is very structured, coming into an environment where you have to make your own structure to be successful. I think that in itself is the biggest difference. That's pretty obvious, but it's also a big challenge for a lot of service members.

Carlos described how living without what he labeled as structure and direction was the biggest challenge for many student veterans, especially for those who had been on active duty. Hence, they had extreme difficulty in managing their time.

Contrasting with previous studies, our study revealed that the loss of structure caused difficulties in SVSM academic adjustment in addition to their daily routines. Unlike the military, faculty members (authority figures) give less structure and fewer directions to students (subordinates) while individual opinions and multiple perspectives are strongly encouraged in classrooms. Therefore, our SVSM participants struggled with academics as they had to navigate their own professors' expectations with little clarification of anticipated class behaviors and assignments. Henry described what it was like for him to adjust to a lack of detailed expectations:

> [I am completely used to] a job where you get told exactly what to do right to your face by someone. There is no come up with your own idea. This is

what needs to be done, do it, and then I go do it and I do it fine. Whereas in college it's more like, you don't get told to do it, it's just implied you need to do it. And it's not always direct, whereas [in the military] it's like go here, do this at this time, bring this with you, be there from this time to this time and then come back. College is like well, we are going to have a paper due, a project due at this time, you should cover this, this, and this, and it just kind of . . . it's on them [students]. A lot of times I feel like veterans get frustrated, myself included, they just need someone to say "hey do this" and then they can go do it. But they are not getting specific, down to the detail instruction.

Not only was it challenging for our participants to create structures and directions for themselves, but it was also difficult for them to engage in common exchanges in an academic environment where students are asked to come up with their own ideas or to dialogue in open discussion or debate. Steven described why this is difficult for veterans:

> The military is its own little world, and generally everybody has the same perspective and . . . even if there are people that you know feel differently, you're not entitled to speak that here [military]. This is the way it is, you're going to do it this way, and we are not going to have discussion.

Coming from a military culture that uses orders and commands to execute a group mission, many SVSM initially are not accustomed to individual and autonomous thinking and to make meaning of diverse perspectives, which are highly valued in academic culture. This point is also recognized by DeSawal (2013) who stated, "the academic rigor of higher education combined with teaching approaches designed to promote reflection and higher-order thinking may create cultural dissonance for student veterans" (p. 79).

Loss of Collectivism

Another impediment our SVSM participants experienced was the loss of the military culture that places a significant importance on strong group identification, group cohesion, and group mission. The academic difficulties described above can also be explained from the perspective of collectivism and individualism. In a collectivist culture, as in the military, hierarchical relationships, roles, and duties are critical elements to effectively accomplish group goals. Yet, in an academic environment rooted in individualism, these essential collectivist cultural components are missing. Therefore, our SVSM participants often struggled in classrooms in college.

In addition, our SVSM participants struggled with the loss of collectivist culture in their social lives on campus. This cultural difference was communicated in subtle ways as they expressed the strong feeling of disconnection that they experienced in the college environment. Manuel said:

> I was pretty much on my own. I would just sit at a corner of the library by myself and read. Once that was done, I pretty much got onto the Internet, walked around, and ate. It seems like it was just me and [then] everyone else on campus.

Like Manuel, many of our SVSM participants described how they felt alone and isolated, and had minimum interactions with other students when they started college. This experience is consistent with McBain et al. (2012) who reported continuing social isolation among the SVSM population. In exploring SVSM social isolation further, our study revealed a strong influence of collectivism that contributed to their social discomfort.

Our study found that there are two ways in which collectivism influenced the SVSM sense of social alienation in the college environment. First, many of our participants felt disconnected as they grieved the loss of camaraderie that they had in the military. Participants described how the strong bonds they established with other military service members were so special and unique that it was hard to replicate those bonds with peers in college. David described the uniqueness of military camaraderie as follows:

> [It's] like understanding that you have other people around you, even if it's the shittiest day in the world, it's like you're all doing the same shit together, and I didn't realize how much I relied on that. So when . . . going to a college and you feel like you're lost in the system . . . you don't have anybody there that's like sitting next to you that has been waiting for the past 12 hours with you, like they kind of look at each other and say "yeah this is a really crappy situation." So I think that was the biggest one . . . that you don't have [that] kind of . . . social support.

In the collectivistic culture of the military, service members rely on strong group identification and unit cohesion as "the important components of combat readiness as individuals must learn to trust group members with their very lives" (Christian et al., 2009, p. 33), and such strong group cohesion serves as a protective factor against stress for the service members (Christian et al., 2009). Therefore, the loss of camaraderie indicated the absence of significant resources familiar to SVSM, especially in their stressful transition from the military to college. Furthermore, as illustrated in David's comments, in the military SVSM participants *always* had their buddies with whom they could share their experiences no matter what was going on in their lives. Therefore, being away from the consistent presence of military camaraderie created a sense of aloneness for many participants. They longed to connect with students with military backgrounds, but many of the participants we interviewed struggled to find other SVSM. For example, Angelina reflected on her start of college in 2006 after her first deployment to Iraq:

> There was just me. That's what it felt like. I know it wasn't, but there was no way to connect to anyone else. You might hear a professor say, "oh, yeah. I have another kid that deployed" or "I have another student that [is a veteran]," but for the most part. . .

Another way that collectivism influenced SVSM social isolation on campus was their own perception of how different they are from civilian students. Steven stated:

> I believe that veterans bring a different perspective . . . a different perspective as far as communication in the classroom, a different perspective as far as the way they carry themselves, and a different perspective as far as pride in the environment.

Like Steven, many of our SVSM participants consistently felt different from other students on campus due to their military experience. This self-perception seems to be a by-product of a strong group orientation in the military where they are trained to think of themselves as different from civilians as they become a part of the military unit, organization, and missions. Also, when individuals identify so strongly with a group, they attribute positive characteristics to their group while assigning negative attributions to other groups (Christian et al., 2009). Given these functions of strong group cohesiveness, educators can begin to appreciate the magnitude of the emotional effects that the loss of camaraderie has on the lives of SVSM on campus.

Loss of Masculinity

Another cultural difference that participants encountered was a college environment that is no longer dominated by a strong emphasis on masculinity and physical prowess as in the military. For instance, some participants struggled with pent-up energy due to a reduced level of physical activity in college in comparison to the high activity level required in the military. Also, coming from a military environment that is dominated by male service members, some participants recognized the need to change their behaviors to be appropriate and sensitive to the female population. Henry's comments illustrate this point:

> I was in the Marines; I was in the infantry, so I lived in the barracks with all guys, so there were no girls. The only time we saw girls were out on the

weekends or if we left for a holiday or something. So that's a nice change. But there are things you get used to doing when you're around nothing but guys that you can't do when you are around normal society.

A female veteran, Angelina, also noted her experience in the male-dominated culture of the military: "I always felt like I was a guy anyway, because all of my units have been male units, so I was used to that [male dominance]." Angelina was living in not only a male-dominated world but also in a military unit where there were few females. Therefore, she had to be assimilated into the male-dominated culture of the military while her male counterparts did not. However, once her male counterparts arrived on college campus, they experienced the need to be acculturated to the college campus with a large female population, what Henry referred to as "normal." Angelina described her observation of male SVSM on her campus:

> I don't think the guys were as used to it [interacting with females] because most of the guys at SVA [Student Veterans Association] were from infantry units, so there were not many female interactions; so they [male veterans] were not prepared for it because they never had to do it.

Angelina gave the following example to illustrate the unpreparedness that some male SVSM exhibited during a group meeting:

> There was an issue with a mixer that they wanted to have. They named it "GI Joes and Army Whores," which made me so angry, because that's the characterization of females in the military to begin with. So we were really angered by that, so they quashed it.

This exemplifies the cultural conflict between male dominance in the military and gender equality in academia. As stated earlier, masculinity comes with ideas of male normalcy and power over women, but these perspectives and behaviors significantly counterbalance aspects of academia that value equality and diversity. To this end, some of our SVSM participants recognized that the masculine norms and behaviors that they adhered to in the military were inappropriate and unwelcome in the college setting. Henry described how a joke that works in the military may not be appropriate in a college environment:

> Little jokes that I would make in the Marine Corps that aren't quite as funny here I guess. Everyone in the Marine Corp is absolutely offensive in every way shape or form to everyone. You can't take offense to it. So I mean we all make fun of each other for anything: your religion, your race, you're fat, you're tall, you're skinny, you're dumb, you're smart, you're major wealthy. It doesn't

matter. We're also very self-loathing so we just make fun of each other's pain and misery, which here you're not supposed to. Insults when they are down, so to speak. So that was a little bit of a transition.

Such teasing and shaming in the military seem to communicate the masculinity of aggression, dominance, and emotional stoicism, which are highly valued and promoted for survival and mission completion (Eisenhart, 1998; Rueb et al., 2008). Henry's comments exemplify the salient transition issues of SVSM students who are working to be successful in an environment that seeks to graduate citizens with individual and autonomous agency. His comments also communicate that as a male Marine it was only "a little bit of a transition."

As described in this section, cultural conflict between the cultures of the military and higher education surfaced in a variety of ways in multiple contexts in the college experience of SVSM. How did SVSM respond to this cultural conflict? In the next section, we use the perspective of acculturation as a lens to organize responses of SVSM to the cultural conflict.

SVSM'S ACCULTURATION TO THE COLLEGE CULTURE

We find that Berry's (2005) model of acculturation offers a theoretical explanation of how SVSM respond to the cultural conflict they experience on college campuses. According to Berry, acculturation is "the dual process of cultural and psychological change that takes place as a result of contact between two or more cultural groups and their individual members" (p. 698). Acculturation is a time-consuming process that involves voluntary mutual changes of individuals in two groups (typically a dominant and subordinate group) and of the culture within the groups. Acculturation can only occur when there is voluntary change in the dominant and subordinate cultural groups and individuals in these groups.

We believe that Berry's (2005) model addresses critical issues in understanding SVSM acculturation to the higher education environment. First, Berry's model takes into account the existence of power differentiation and dynamics between SVSM (non-dominant group) and higher education (dominant group). Therefore, this model allows for recognizing the significant role that the members and the climate of the college play in the acculturation of SVSM into the higher education context. Also, this model offers various approaches that SVSM can use to acculturate in the college environment by considering the following underlying dimensions of their acculturation: (a) the way in which SVSM maintain cultural aspects of the military in college; (b) how SVSM connect with the higher education culture; and (c) the degree to which SVSM participate in the culture of higher education. Below we describe acculturation strategies of both SVSM

35

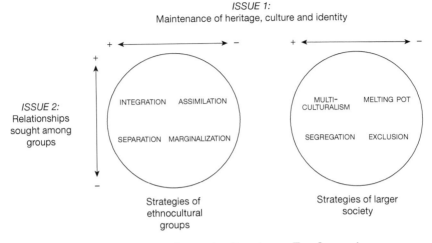

ISSUE 1:
Maintenance of heritage, culture and identity

ISSUE 2:
Relationships
sought among
groups

INTEGRATION   ASSIMILATION

SEPARATION   MARGINALIZATION

MULTI-   MELTING POT
CULTURALISM

SEGREGATION   EXCLUSION

Strategies of
ethnocultural
groups

Strategies of larger
society

Figure 2.1 Four Acculturation Strategies Based upon Two Issues, in
Ethnocultural Groups and the Larger Society

Source: From Berry, J. W. (2005) "Acculturation: Living Successfully in Two Cultures," *International Journal of Intercultural Relations, 29,* p. 705. Copyright 2005 by Elsevier. Reprinted with permission.

(non-dominant group) and higher education (dominant group) using Berry's model.

As illustrated in Figure 2.1, Berry (1980) developed four sets of acculturation strategies based on two issues that are concerns for all acculturating individuals: (a) orientation towards one's own cultural group; and (b) alignment towards other groups. These sets of strategies are *assimilation/melting pot, separation/ segregation, marginalization/exclusion,* and *integration/multiculturalism.* Applying Berry's model to SVSM acculturation to college, *assimilation* is when SVSM do not want to retain their military cultural identities but seek to actively engage with the college culture. When assimilation is expected by the college environment, it is referred to as *melting pot.* In contrast, *separation* is when SVSM individuals wish to hold on to military culture while avoiding engagement with the college culture. When separation is expected by the members of the college, it is called *segregation. Marginalization* is when there is little possibility of or interest in SVSM maintaining the military culture or making a connection with the college culture. Marginalization becomes *exclusion* when it is forced by the dominant college culture. *Integration* occurs when SVSM are interested in maintaining the military culture as well as interacting with the college culture. Integration becomes *multiculturalism* when diversity is an accepted value of the college environment.

In our study, many participants tried to engage in the process of integration in their acculturation to the college environment: they tried to maintain the

36

military culture while participating in the college culture. Two aspects of the military culture that many of our SVSM participants attempted to maintain were the rigid hierarchical social structure and a strong sense of military camaraderie through recreating these features in their student lives. This was usually accomplished by consistently searching for military-style leadership that provides clear direction and a means to navigate through the ambiguity they felt in the culture of academia. Therefore, our participants actively sought out interactions to recreate this military cultural framework. Henry described how he lured a faculty member into giving him the instructions he needed to complete academic assignments:

> I'll go to the professor after the class, and [I'll] be like, "Ok, tell me what can I do" and a lot of times they [professors] will still give me the idea they want me to think. Once you lure them in to telling what you need to do, you can kind of get that conversation started and eventually they will tell you what you need to do and then I can go and do it.

To manipulate faculty to mimic the leadership that he used to follow in the military, Henry frequently visited his professors and obtained the detailed directions he was used to. Only then was Henry able to complete his academic assignments.

Developing camaraderie with other SVSM was another way that many participants tried to recreate the military culture in their college lives. Many noted that meeting other SVSM was significantly helpful in their acculturation to college. To establish this sense of camaraderie, some participants already had arranged to come to the college with their buddies from the military, and they lived together and supported each other throughout college. Many others who came to college alone sought to identify other SVSM. David described how he met other veterans as follows:

> I was looking for other veterans, and I had posted on that little tab like, "Are there any veterans still here?" She sent me an email through my college email address, and she said, "Let's meet at some point. I got three other people that want to come too." So we met for lunch one day, and she was great. We're still friends.

Like David, many participants struggled to find other SVSM on campus, especially if they attended colleges that have not established student organizations or clubs for SVSM. College environments that lacked the support to maintain the cultural identity of SVSM present the melting pot of Berry's model; thus, SVSM in these colleges faced the contextual and implicit pressure by the university to assimilate into the college environment.

However, instead of being expected to assimilate, when there was no support for SVSM on campus, many of our participants took matters into their own hands to create a change. Many began to advocate for their need to maintain their military cultural identities. For instance David established an opportunity for military camaraderie by creating a social support group for veterans:

> When I got here, there wasn't any kind of veteran support at all. And then, I randomly got an email from somebody one day. That was like "Hey I'm a veteran and I want to start a group" and I was like "This is fantastic. What's up?"

Not every campus provided support for SVSM who attempted to maintain their cultural identities. Manuel explained the difficulties he encountered in his attempt to create a supportive environment for student veterans on his campus:

> We just have to fight administrators for things you want, and they don't understand why . . . we had to fight for a veterans' lounge. We had to explain why it was necessary. Soldiers and military [people] come here and don't really relate with people on campus, and need somewhere to study or relax and not to feel the difference.

The unsupportive attitudes exhibited by Manuel's school administrators indicate the presence of segregation, which in turn encourages SVSM to adopt a strategy of separation. According to Berry (2005), individuals experiencing segregation avoid cultural conflict by withdrawing from participating in their acculturation context. The following comments by Jerry, who also worked with Manuel, illustrate separation/segregation strategy and "turn their back on involvement with other cultural groups" (Berry, 2005, p. 705).

> [We felt a] general sense of isolation and frustration with the administration and university . . . the lack of respect that we were feeling. We needed to do something about it, so we started having meetings more. We decided that we were not trying to rely on the school anymore.

When the campus expected SVSM to separate, what did SVSM do? In our study, the frustration experienced by the SVSM was transformed into energy for aggressively executing an advocacy mission of creating a veteran-friendly campus. Moreover, this mission provided an opportunity for the SVSM participants to utilize the skills that they had learned in the military. Michael described his advocacy strategies as follows:

> Some of the tactics that we used was stuff that I learned in the Seals; right away I bypassed gate keepers [to get to] the senior executives in my school.

38

So, we dressed up in suits and ties and *ambushed* them there and used the leverage.

To avoid cultural conflict, Michael seemed to "turn inward toward their heritage culture" (Berry, 2005, p. 705) of the military and relied on masculinity to fight with his unsupportive college to execute his advocacy mission.

In our study, a significant problem that contributed to an unsupportive campus environment was a lack of communication between administrators and SVSM. This absence of meaningful dialogue often led to misunderstandings. Not allowing SVSM a space for connecting with their military culture was seen by SVSM as an act of exclusion by the university. Thus, it forced SVSM to opt for marginalization which promotes "feelings of non-engagement or attachment to either group" (p. 707). In fact, studies of acculturative stress have consistently reported that marginalization is the most stressful strategy for acculturation (Berry, 2005); thus, this strategy should be avoided.

In contrast, integration is the least stressful strategy for acculturation (Berry, 2005), yet it requires mutual agreement and accommodations between SVSM and the college for the acculturation strategy to follow. Moreover, the ability of SVSM to choose this strategy is only possible when the academic environment embraces a multicultural orientation that fosters integration of SVSM into the college culture. In our study, the key to creating a context of multiculturalism to support a SVSM integration strategy is the university's commitment to provide needed services for SVSM. In addition to military-friendly policies and support services, our participants named specific student affairs professionals, higher education administrators, faculty, and staff who reached out to SVSM and gave them extraordinary support for their acculturation to college. Those individuals became the anchor as participants navigated the unfamiliar culture of academia. They also understood how difficult the transition from the military to higher education is, they had cultural sensitivity towards the military culture, and they taught SVSM the culture of academia. They also appreciated the unique perspectives that SVSM bring to the campus and helped them to integrate into the college environment. The following comments by Stan, a director of the veterans' services office, illustrate the multicultural strategy endorsed by the college:

> We think it's important that veterans are fully integrated into life here at the university, but it's equally important that they share an experience that less than 1% of the American public has experienced. I mean, less than 1% served our nation in uniform. So they bring to the university a whole set of experiences that are really worth sharing.

His comments clearly demonstrate that the university welcomes the diversity that SVSM brings to the campus community.

For those participants whose campus already established special support for SVSM, the campus veterans services office became the oasis where they could reconnect with the military culture on their college campus. Thus, when feeling lost in college, they visited the campus veterans services office to obtain clear structures and directions. Steven described helpful support that he received at the veterans services office at his college:

> "This is your first step, this is your second step, this is your third step; if at any time in this process you get lost come right back to this office and we will re-orient you and point you in the right direction." In a lot of ways it's helpful to me because I still interact with military-type people. Because after being 21 years in the military and leaving that environment, it's kind of a culture shock.

By visiting the campus veterans' services office, which provided clear structures and detailed directions, Steven was able to fulfill his need to recreate the military culture.

Berry (2005) stated, "As a result of attempts to cope with these acculturation changes, some long-term adaptations may be achieved" (p. 709). Indeed, many of our participants discussed how they learned to adapt to college despite the cultural conflicts described above. Although the loss of rigid structures initially appeared as the most challenging aspect that SVSM experience in their transition to college, many of our SVSM participants dealt with this cultural conflict through cultural learning and selectively incorporated new behaviors that fit with the academic environment. This change represents sociocultural adaption that indicates one's ability to manage everyday life in a new cultural context (Ward, 1996). Social adaptation usually improves over time in a linear fashion and is enhanced by cultural knowledge, degree of contact, and positive intergroup attitudes (Berry, 2005). In adapting to the academic cultural context, SVSM also integrated the approaches used in the military when appropriate. For instance, Henry used military leadership appropriately in his class: "I think [classmates] needed direction and someone to tell them what to do. So I brought a little bit of order and structure to our class project." Henry's comment illustrates the use of integration strategy as it involves the selective adaptation of new behaviors from the college culture, as well as the retention of valued features of his military culture.

Unlike the loss of structure that participants adopted to over time, camaraderie was the aspect of the military culture that many of our SVSM participants actively maintained throughout their acculturation to the college. Many participants in our study found that joining the student veteran organization was tremendously beneficial. Examples of their comments are as follows:

We're a lot older and we have some words and stories we say that nobody understands. Like I could tell you a boot camp story and you probably wouldn't find that as funny as another Marine would, and certain jokes only work with other veterans.

(Miguel)

With veterans, you can talk about deployment, different issues, like some people had like deep issues with deployment. So you have people to sit down and talk to.

(Alan)

I learned that a lot of us felt the same way. We all felt and experienced the same things . . . just like . . . general sense of isolation and frustration with the administration and university . . . just a lack of respect that we were feeling.

(Jerry)

As illustrated in the above comments, recreating military camaraderie provided a special space for participants to feel a sense of belonging, share and affirm their unique perspectives, obtain emotional support, and help accomplish their mission in college. This social support is vital in the process of acculturation as it facilitates psychological adaptation related to one's physical and mental well-being in a new cultural context (Ward, 1996).

Through successfully navigating the challenges they faced in the unfamiliar culture of college, many participants also began to understand and appreciate the cultural values embedded in academia. Although they struggled at the beginning, many noted that their views have been broadened because of their academic experience. This change also indicates better psychological adaptation noted above. For instance, Miguel discussed how his views about women in the military changed as he was exposed to different perspectives in academia:

The military is predominantly male, they have their own stereotypes about females in the military . . . as far as physical fitness and stuff like that, and just women in combat, they have this perspective that perhaps women can't do it. [Now] being a social justice minor, I see that it's not gender specific. Women can do these things, it's just giving [them] the opportunity. As soon as all these ideas are coming, my perspective starts changing. There are a lot of things that the school throws that just adds to my perspective.

Indeed, many participants talked about new learning and new perspectives that they gained through their college experience. In other words, navigating the cultural conflict offered an opportunity for many of our SVSM participants to broaden their perspectives. Through acculturating to a college environment that values individualism, diversity, and freedom of expression, SVSM also found a way to reconcile what appeared to be contradicting values of the military and college. Steven summarized this point beautifully:

> I learned that going to college is about teaching you to see things differently . . . being able to grasp different perspectives and other points of view. Not that you necessarily agree with it, but that you acknowledge that it's there and that you recognize that there are differences. I personally have grown through seeing and hearing other people's perspectives.

CONCLUSION

In this chapter, we examined the cultural contexts that influence SVSM experience in college. The cultures of the U.S. military and U.S. higher education are significantly different. Therefore, SVSM experienced cultural dissonance in their transition from the military to college. SVSM used various strategies to acculturate to the college environment. However, not all colleges provided a supportive context for SVSM to successfully transition from their military culture into their new college setting. What can higher education administrators and student affairs professionals learn from the cultural navigation of SVSM?

First and foremost, administrators, educators, and practitioners must understand and appreciate the unique culture of the military as well as the influence of the military culture on the experiences of SVSM in college. Indeed, a number of military scholars argue that it is impossible to fully understand the psychological experience of military service members without understanding the cultural values of the military (Christian et al., 2009). Therefore, higher education administrators and student affairs professionals must obtain additional training and consultation to develop multicultural competencies to work effectively with the SVSM population. Also, to be culturally competent, administrators and practitioners must be aware of their own assumptions, biases, and stereotypes toward the military culture while at the same time acknowledging their own cultures, including the culture of U.S. higher education to which they belong.

Applying Berry's (2005) acculturation model, higher education administrators and student affairs professionals can establish or modify a program to support SVSM's cultural transition to college. For instance, student affairs professionals can introduce the notion of culture shock as a framework for SVSM to reflect on the military culture, the culture of academia, and how they experience and respond to the clash between these cultures. Then, student affairs practitioners can describe the process of acculturation, including strategies, acculturative stress, and psychological and social outcomes. To illustrate the clash between collectivist and individualistic cultures, student affairs practitioners even reference the transitional experiences of international students from strong collectivist cultures (i.e. China, Mexico, Pakistan, etc.) and their acculturation to the environment of U.S. higher education. This may help SVSM to relate with other student populations on their campus. These types of efforts can encourage SVSM to better manage acculturative stress by empowering them to make informed decisions about how they want to respond to cultural conflicts faced in college.

Finally, as members of the dominant group in the context of higher education, administrators and student affairs professionals possess significant power and resources to create a multicultural context that facilitates SVSM's integration into college. Thus, administrators and practitioners must act as advocates to create a campus environment that embraces diverse cultures including the military culture. SVSM advocacy is detailed in Chapter 4. But before persons can advocate, we believe they must be facilitators. We identify facilitator characteristics and behaviors next.

Chapter 3

Facilitators and Barriers to Success

During our data collection process, Glen, the student affairs vice president at RI told us:

> For about a year or so I pulled together everybody and tried to work through these issues [poor support practices of SVSM]. My main goal was to find somebody who knew more about veterans' issues than I did, because I was knowledgeable but by no means had the expertise to pull off veterans' services. For me this became an issue of recognizing that veterans are a special population not unlike other populations we have. Because they are special populations we need to provide special services.

As mentioned in the previous chapter, our study sought to expand the knowledge about college experiences of SVSM. We employed a multi-site case study methodology to explore: (a) the experiences of student affairs professionals, administrators, and students (non-military and military) in creating and maintaining a military friendly campus; (b) facilitators and barriers to student veteran learning and engagement; and (c) differing practices that meet student needs and demonstrate institutional commitment. This chapter focuses specifically on our research findings of leadership actions that moved institutions to recognize the need for and then to provide special services for SVSM. If it is true that "institutional leaders, from presidents and provosts to vice presidents and deans, are critical to the success of establishment of and support for student veteran services" (Jackson, Fey, & Ross, 2013, p. 255), then how do institutional leaders come to recognize the need for change and specifically how did institution leaders in our study create change to better facilitate SVSM success? According to the *Advanced English Dictionary* (2014), to *facilitate* is to make something easier. A facilitator is someone who prompts progress by increasing the likelihood that others act in useful ways. In this chapter we delve into the nature of facilitating success for special populations in higher education, particularly the SVSM population. What did Glen and others do to facilitate SVSM success? How did they overcome barriers? First, we describe the sites of our study. Then, we offer how context influences serving SVSM at our study sites. This is followed by a discussion of the nature of complex problem recognition and complex problem solving. We then use complex problem solving as an avenue for identifying practices that facilitate SVSM success.

STUDY SITES

To determine study sites for our multi-site case study, we asked a purposeful sample of student affairs and higher education educators to recommend institutions which they thought were responding well to the needs of SVSM. Because there is too little research in higher education published about community colleges, we wanted one of our sites to be a community college. Hence, we selected two public institutions, one a community college (CC) and one a research-extensive institution (RI). Both were institutions well recognized for their efforts in meeting the needs of SVSM. In fact, the community college had never stopped offering campus veterans' services from the Vietnam era, though staffing for campus veterans' services increased in light of the armed conflicts in Iraq and Afghanistan.

Coincidentally, both institutions had multiple campuses and both institutions had previously identified one campus as a main campus with other campuses deemed satellite campuses. However, both institutions had taken measures to decentralize some organizational and administrative functions to de-emphasize the satellite perception. In other words, both institutions sought to communicate that there was no longer a "main campus," but rather the institution had multiple, equally important campuses. However, at both institutions there were more veterans services staff physically located and more veterans' services offered at the campus that was once considered the institution's "main campus."

In recognizing the differences of these institutions, it is beneficial to dissect how these differences affect facilitating the success of SVSM. What does facilitating a SVSM student population look like at these two different institutions?

INSTITUTIONAL CONTEXT

Summarizing research on institutional diversity efforts, Milem, Chang, and Antonio (2005) identified five interconnected dimensions that lead to educational benefits for students. These dimensions include compositional diversity, historical legacy of inclusion or exclusion, psychological climate, behavioral climate, and organizational structure (or how embedded into institutional processes such as the curriculum, reward structures, and admissions practices is the value of diversity). In this chapter we use these dimensions as a framework through which

45

to describe institutional and individual practices that serve as facilitators or barriers to engagement of SVSM in the campus community. The rural nature of some of the CC campuses as compared to the urban locations of all of the RI campuses influences the differences in their demographic composition. So too does the very nature of the two institutions. The open access mission of CC in conjunction with its pervasive mission to serve an adult population made it a viable institution to attract the SVSM population from its inception. With its emphasis on graduate education and the selective admission of its undergraduates, RI had not previously identified itself as an institution that could or should cater to SVSM, but once academically talented SVSM began to attend in sufficient numbers, those students asked to be noticed.

The pre-college experiences of students shape their expectations of campus life (Pope & LePeau, 2012). Milem et al.'s (2005) framework concludes that students who see a noticeable number of students, faculty, and staff on campus like them and see that there are programs that seek to recruit and retain people like them are more likely to be engaged in the institution. Furthermore, feelings of belonging are promoted when issues they care about are included in the curriculum and in official institutional statements. Hence, if there seem to be few SVSM on campus, if their values or assumptions seem contrary to that of the campus culture, and if they are either absent from the curriculum and institution documents or misunderstood in the curriculum and institution documents, then they will most likely resist engaging in the institution. Again, because CC operated a veterans services office with veteran employees (though only part-time until after the Iraq and Afghanistan conflicts began) and RI did not, there was a stark contrast in how SVSM felt they belonged to their respective institutions as the numbers of veterans increased at both (an example of Milem et al.'s (2005) historical legacy of inclusion or exclusion dimension). The CC SVSM alumni we spoke with felt connected to the institution, but current SVSM students at RI could recall feeling disconnected and isolated. Because students at RI tended to be more politically active than at CC, there was a larger anti-war presence at RI. Unfortunately this was experienced by veterans as an anti-veteran presence.

Student engagement is influenced by "the cues they receive from faculty and peers" (Pope & LePeau, 2012, p. 115). Harper and Quaye (2009) called upon higher education administrators, student affairs practitioners, staff, students, and faculty to continually reflect on and dialogue about the assumptions they bring with them to campus. These dialogues should promote a deeper, more mutual understanding. At both CC and RI, we uncovered evidence that meaningful dialogues had taken place to encourage mutual understanding. At RI, however, it meant a revision of who a special population is and how to better serve them. We believe this necessitated complex problem solving.

COMPLEX PROBLEM SOLVING

RI had no comprehensive coordination of SVSM services prior to 9/11. As Glen's quote that opened this chapter illustrated, changing the campus to one that cared about and served SVSM began with the recognition that there was a problem. In general, prior to problem solving there must be problem recognition. Weick (2005) defined sense-making as creating a new interpretation that does not yet have a name. In the quote above, Glen, a vice president at RI, recognized veterans as a special population not unlike other special populations. Prior to that recognition, we believe Glen observed circumstances that did not have a name, but he came to name as a "special population." What prompted Glen to this recognition?

Glen's leadership position may have allowed him freedom to identify hints of new patterns in the fabric of campus life. Weick (2005) believed such new interpretations tend not to come from coordinators or mid-level managers because they are too preoccupied with managing "in-family events" (p. 426) or familiar reoccurring responsibilities that are mired in habitual assumptions. This discourages imaginative thinking because repetitive responsibilities deter considering the nuances that appear in new patterns. According to McCormack (2009) and Weick (2005), the problem solver is as much a factor in problem solving as the problem itself. McCormack wrote, "our relationship with the problem could be crucial inasmuch as we identify as problem solvers . . . We might say that we are what (or whom) we solve" (p. 19). Glen's self-identity as a problem solver enabled him to recognize a problem. Welch (2007) advanced that it is intuition that allows for the recognition of a problem. Complex problem solvers employ "impressions, hunches, and feelings" (Birgerstam, 2002, p. 431) and use intuition to "gaze upon" and "contemplate" (p. 432). It is intuition that offers the creative ability to notice a change in a pattern and refrain from classifying it; a suspension of judgment is required. Birgerstam (2002) argued that both intuition and reason are crucial to problem solving, but that reason often leads to reductionism whereas intuition prompts nuanced or "non-obvious relationships" (p. 137) to be discovered and explored. Reason employs a different kind of knowledge than intuition. Reason could inform administrators that the number of SVSM is a small portion of the student population. Reason would also inform administrators that SVSM could be defined as a privileged population (primarily male and White) coming to campus with military educational benefits (additional privilege). However, according to Birgerstam those who use intuition "occupy ourselves with the present, continuous flow of impressions concerning unverifiable truths and untruths" (p. 431, italics in original). We believe that intuition influenced Glen's recognition that the numbers of SVSM should be a "servant, not a master, to intuition" (Birgerstam, 2002, p. 432). Glen recognized that SVSM seemed to be in trouble, but he had no data on which to confirm his

47

hunches. How to respond to intuition must be guided by critical thought that includes feedback (Welch, 2007). Hence, reason and intuition can coalesce into greater understanding.

As we will discuss in more detail below, some educators did not recognize the new pattern that intuition offers. This might be because of a reluctance to risk acting on a hunch, lack of positional power to think and do something differently, the inability to recognize nuanced patterns, or the belief that current practice is sufficient. Yet, Jackson et al. (2013) argued that campus leaders have the obligation to "seize opportunities to ensure that individual student veterans and service members have the services and program necessary to make the most of a potentially life-changing experience" (p. 256). Jackson et al. believed accomplishing that depends on the number of SVSM, the potential to grow this population, number of nearby military installations, the values of the state legislature, and the expectations of current students. How did RI capitalize on opportunities to prompt poignant learning experiences for SVSM?

INSTITUTIONALIZING SYSTEMS

As highlighted in the quote opening this chapter, Glen's recognition of SVSM as a special population was pivotal to initiating subsequent actions that enhanced SVSM success on campus. He understood that SVSM have some of the same experiences, needs, and feelings of other students but that they also have unique ones as well. Glen believed the institution had an obligation to enable students to "find a community that supports who you are and recognizes that it is an important part of how they form their identity, and also how they come to understand themselves" (an example of Milem et al.'s (2005) behavioral climate dimension).

As SVSM were voicing concerns that the institution was not providing the services or support necessary for SVSM "to survive" and "move forward," Glen was bringing together leaders across campus to make recommendations on what the institution should do to better support SVSM. Because a president's involvement sends a signal to the community that this is an institutional priority (Jackson et al., 2013), the concurrence of RI's president with all the recommendations made by Glen's task force expedited the process for making them happen. This process transformed the institution from one with little attention paid to SVSM to an institution lauded for its focus on SVSM (an example of Milem et al.'s (2005) organizational dimension). What was this process? How does an institution come to address the needs of a special population, and in particular a SVSM one?

First, Glen established a permanent advisory committee for campus veterans services composed of dedicated staff, faculty, and administrators from across the institution as well as experts from outside the institution. Glen thought it was important that he chair this group, not to control it but to model its significance. Next, Glen looked for expert staff he could bring to campus. He noted, "Really, to see what can happen under the leadership of somebody that really understands veteran services is quite amazing." Glen ensured that staff assisting SVSM represented both enlisted and officer personnel, a wide age range, and different branches. According to Glen "[we created] a remarkably good team." Establishing a community of SVSM that provided an opportunity to connect with each other was a priority. Glen exclaimed:

> I saw it as my job to make sure these students had a positive experience, being able to connect in a community and could really become a part of us as an institution so we could invest in their success.

Therefore, he "mobilized resources to pull that together." Such efforts "institutionalize the initiative throughout the campus" (Jackson et al., 2013, p. 259). RI quickly responded to the needs Glen's advisory committee identified. Stan, a member of the task force who later became the director of veterans services, described the group as one with "sufficient muscle to actually make policy changes." The task force drew together "small pieces" that had already been established across campus. According to Glen, "We pulled together resources and made commitments from experts that already existed here."

Not knowing the extent of SVSM isolation was of considerable concern to Glen. He longed to compare his hunches with data. Changes to the institution's admission application and other practices served to track SVSM and discover their retention, persistence, and graduation rates as well as other vital information.

Another early initiative was to create a "one-stop shop" in a renovated space at what historically was considered its main campus. According to Glen, this one-stop office was tasked with "making sure that every one of these students [veterans] gets what he or she needs in order to be successful." This included office hours by a career and personal counselor and tutoring services by student volunteers. Having drop-in academic advisor hours was also desirable, but the dean of advising said he was too short-staffed. Instead, the dean agreed to offer hours himself. Interestingly, Stan claimed that they made the best coffee there, which is not unimportant.

More importantly, Glen told us that "it's easy to get lost here, this is a difficult place. But our leaders make it easy for students to be found." For example, some student veterans arrive on campus

> desperate, they don't have money, they don't know how to apply for benefits or weren't applying for the benefits. In one case, somebody was homeless. [Our campus veterans' services director] mobilized resources on the campus, found a place for the person to live. People excused the rent that he had to

pay until he could pay it. Basically [the director] made exceptions. He got [the student] enrolled, got him a house, got him a food plan.

This story exemplifies how veterans have become members of a special population deserving special consideration from the institution and the federal government due to their service to their country. Glen commented that SVSM do bring with them to RI educational benefits that are a source of income, "but in [our state] we had a commitment to make these people that had dedicated part of their lives to protecting others . . . a moral obligation." This begs the question, however, of the ability of other populations on campus to have such needs addressed. If this student was not a student veteran would there have been a mobilization of assistance? How many other homeless students, veterans or non-veterans, are unidentified and underserved?

This state commitment prompted campus leaders to grow the SVSM enrollment, both undergraduate and graduate (an example of Milem et al.'s (2005) compositional diversity dimension). The director of campus veterans' services, in conjunction with the vice president for enrollment and the vice president for budget and finance, believed that the institution would "attract high caliber people that were highly motivated." They established a goal to enable SVSM to hear about RI before leaving the military. Stan relayed that he received a call from a Marine Corp guard at the American Embassy in the Ukraine who said "somebody told me to call you about getting into RI." Campus leaders created a plan to increase the number of SVSM from a meager 300 to an eventual 1,500. That included sending applicants a letter from the campus veterans services office and marketing with the state legislature.

Such increases in the student population affect the campus culture. As discussed in Chapter 2, when different cultures congregate, they influence each other. RI is no exception. The increased presence of SVSM put real faces to the war debate. Campus leaders felt that students and faculty have come to a greater awareness of war and society that is less abstract. According to Stan, the greatest institutional accomplishment was to "separate the policy of the [Iraq] war from the person who was told to go fight the war." He also felt that SVSM engagement in the campus community better educated the U.S. public on an experience that less than 1% of the population shares.

One of the most important findings in our study was that institutional leadership makes a significant difference in how campuses respond to special populations. Calls for assistance by SVSM were met with different reactions from RI's various campuses. At one campus without the one-stop student veterans services office we saw how strong leadership and a commitment by a number of dedicated employees with other full-time positions can make a significant difference in the lives of SVSM. We call this campus the Little Engine that Could.

The Little Engine that Could

RI tasked each campus to address the needs of SVSM. At one campus without the campus veterans' services office, a task force was established that included members from the registrar's office, alumni affairs, financial aid, counseling center, and health center as well as the student veterans' club advisor. Also, a graduate academic dean and an academic associate dean were members. The task force was chaired by this campus's senior student affairs officer, Arthur. The group was able to create campus systems that made for easier navigation of the campus by SVSM. Priorities included more assistance with certifying veterans' benefits and financial aid, creating a community of SVSM, and connecting SVSM to the campus at large. These systems were accomplished with only an additional $12,000. This group helped students create a club, lounge, library, and events. At their regularly scheduled meetings, the task force brings forward the names of individual veterans who are in need of assistance. Arthur stated that "we circle the wagons" and "serve as a resource, a network really to bounce off ideas and talk about trends we see occurring." This system demonstrates the desire to recognize nuanced patterns of possible problems that McCormack (2009) and Weick (2005) referred to. Arthur said the group "reinvented the whole veterans initiative" to meet this campus's needs. The group "helps [students] discover how to navigate the complexities of just life." For example, the group loaned money to student veterans whose benefits have not yet been received. Also, in learning that a student who was the spouse of a deployed service member had attempted suicide, the graduate dean visited the student in the hospital and brought back to the group questions regarding family stress and possible ways of offering increased support. Both student veterans and staff at this campus discussed how difficult dialogues had occurred over a proposed program. Though Arthur felt strongly that the program should occur, he respected the wishes of the student veterans' club members and allowed them to decide. Arthur disclosed, "You know, I'm only processing it from an administrator and programmer . . . I'm only processing it from that area. If I were a veteran it would be different." It was clear that Arthur and the staff and faculty at this RI campus offered services to address needs, but also acknowledged that the student veterans needed to control how their story was told. He acknowledged that in some sense there was a disconnect between him and student veterans at this campus, but there was also a connection. The disconnection was with him, the administrator non-veteran, whereas the connection was with him, the caring human being. It was obvious during our visit here that there was much care and respect between SVSM and student affairs practitioners, higher education administrators, faculty, and staff in the advisory group. Discussions of this care frequently led to deep expressions of gratitude from and to students. We were honored to be a part of one of their discussions.

The campus we named The Little Engine that Could is an example of what a group of devoted people with committed leadership can do. We felt it was no accident that a number of members of the advisory committee were people of color. It is obvious that working with students who were advocating for themselves was something they were used to, felt comfortable with, and even promoted. Furthermore, poignantly Arthur realized that he didn't know enough about SVSM so attended training and from that "gained a benchmark." But too, he realized that he couldn't serve SVSM by himself. He asked for others to assist who "answered the call." Such vulnerability is not always apparent in campus leaders. We believe this demonstrated the power of servant leadership. However, not all campuses embrace such leadership.

The Engine that Couldn't

From our initial document review, even before arriving at RI, we heard of the concerns SVSM had at one of their campuses. Unlike the other campuses we visited at RI, students here complained about administrators not taking or returning their calls. SVSM experienced administrators as very unsupportive of establishing a student veterans' club. Moreover, at campus events, SVSM told us that they were asked not to speak. Administrators at this campus refused to meet with us, but students from that campus did as well as staff and administrators from other campuses. Arthur noted:

> The whole initiative, the veterans' movement, the student veterans' movement was prompted by the students at [that campus]. [Students] really did push buttons. We have a number of different questions and challenges and accommodations they are still trying to make there. It's the manner in which we approach one another here and have a dialogue. Somewhere down the line their relationship has gotten skewed because they are not communicating effectively. That is not what is happening here.

From these stark contrasting campus practices and the overall initiatives at RI, and those too at CC, what can educators learn?

FACILITATORS

We highlight here the practices and educator characteristics we found that facilitate student engagement.

Campus leaders will need to ensure that SVSM at each campus have access to knowledgeable and caring resources, particularly regarding GI benefits and financial aid. As revealed here, training of campus leaders, faculty, student affairs

Table 3.1 Examples of Facilitator Behaviors

Facilitator Behaviors

- Contemplate the discovery of possible new patterns and nuances
- Respond to the need for students to develop their identity with like others
- Serving SVSM is a priority of the institution and its leadership
- Gather together entities who care about and are already working with SVSM
- Create an advisory committee that meets on a regular basis, discusses trends, and assists individuals in need
- Call upon the extensive institution and state-wide network to assist students
- Admit to what is not known by the institution and create means to find out
- Pay attention to students' academic needs and the academic mission of the institution
- Allow students opportunities to tell their own story
- Create expectations through the institution's reputation
- Maintain relationships with students even when disagreeing or in conflicts
- Offer regular opportunities for higher education employee professional development about SVSM
- Reflect campus culture and context when serving SVSM
- Pay attention to the first impressions of SVSM

practitioners, higher education administrators, and staff is paramount to the successful navigation of the campus by SVSM. Jackson et al. (2103) reminded educators that there are generational differences in veterans' experiences. Training is essential for everyone, not only non-veterans. Furthermore, particular people should be appointed with specific responsibilities to coordinate services and offer opportunities for those involved with and who care about SVSM. A coordinating group should meet on a regular basis. One-stop veteran services offices should be inclusive and directly connect with aspects vital to the academic mission such as academic advising and tutoring. Those poised with particular responsibilities to work with SVSM must be able to call upon their extensive networks to assist students. They must know the institutional systems including where the resources are and how to obtain them when circumstances require it. They must also have a baseline knowledge about the military and GI Bill benefits.

Serving SVSM quickly is essential. In fact, several students at RI stated that they submitted their applications, were accepted, and confirmed their GI Bill benefits all within one week. Because of advances in technology, one RI prospective student met a campus veterans services assistant director at a college fair and had submitted the online application before the assistant director returned to his office.

Facilitators are people and practices that not only support SVSM but do so proactively. This means moving the institution in ways to meet the needs of SVSM. Whether campuses have a one-stop veterans services office or not, an open door policy is essential. It is imperative that all students feel like they are not just a number. Moreover, we found that allowing students to make their own decisions and have control over their own stories leads to their learning and success.

Institutions must create flexible systems that take advantage of the institution's culture. At CC, a yellow check sheet had been created that provided concrete instructions for what students needed to complete. This "yellow sheet" became part of the SVSM's lingo and lore. Participants at CC all mentioned the "yellow sheet." Also at CC, the work–study veteran students served as a knowledgeable peer support for other students and staff. The position offered learning as well as financial benefits for those student veterans who served in those roles. Work–study veterans were seen as knowledgeable experts across the institution. RI utilized other means of support and advocacy, particularly advisory groups and veteran student clubs. CC had no veteran student clubs. This demonstrates that institutions can take advantage of their own cultural assets to serve special populations.

We heard repeatedly that institutional reputation matters. Students at CC had heard about the ongoing efforts to serve SVSM even before they enrolled. At RI, students had heard of its academic rigor and once its one-stop veterans services office was created, they too began to hear of those services. The veteran network is highly developed and institutional reputations are discussed on military installations across the globe.

Though resources are certainly welcome and useful, good work can be accomplished with few additional resources. Administrators must be thoughtful about when and how to use precious resources. Hence, knowledge of local, state, as well as national resources is useful.

The first person SVSM meet on campus serves as a lens to the institution. Unlike many other prospective students, for SVSM this first person is not typically someone in admissions. Instead it would more likely be a certifying official, someone in financial aid, or someone in campus veterans services. One advantage to the Little Engine that Could campus was its certifying officer. We repeatedly heard that she was not only genuinely welcoming but also exceptionally informative. She made an unforgettable caring first impression.

BARRIERS

Mistrust between SVSM and student affairs practitioners, higher education administrators, faculty, and staff creates barriers. We uncovered student perceptions of administrators not answering their emails or returning their phone calls. Students also found administrators acting unprofessionally by talking negatively about them to other students, which then led to conflict. This is unlike Arthur's philosophy that educators should be undeterred by conflict. They should remain in relationships with students with whom they disagree. How else can understanding occur?

Other barriers to effective SVSM transition included offering little opportunity for them to immerse with each other, or even having practices and space policies that prevent such immersion. Ironically, these practices only serve to reinforce SVSM stigmatization. There is substantial evidence in the higher education and student affairs literature verifying how having connections to like-others allows confidence upon which to build and establish connections with different-others, especially within a new environment (Chickering & Reisser, 1994; Helms, 1990; Tinto, 1993). It is with these diverse others that significant learning gains are made (Kuh, Kinzie, Schuh, & Whitt, 2010).

Uninformed staff is another considerable barrier. We encountered staff who did not know the year of when 9/11 occurred and who couldn't differentiate the branches of the military. Misunderstanding of FERPA and confusion between privacy and confidentiality also created barriers to thoughtful practice.

The complexity of modern campuses also provides barriers to learning and successful transitions. Traversing various campuses to take classes and consult needed resources in addition to navigating complex federal government and VA policies can be daunting. Campus employees who are unable to be patient with students as they navigate these complexities serve as a barrier to effective student transition. This is especially the case when considering the extreme potential for lost paperwork in these bureaucracies.

CONCLUSION

Our findings highlight the importance of institutions paying attention to Milem et al.'s (2005) five dimensions of campus environment. At RI complex problem solving led to institutionalizing systems that increased the compositional diversity, changed the historical legacy of inclusion for SVSM, influenced the psychological and behavioral climates, and altered the organizational diversity.

Our findings brought clarification about problem solving, skills and characteristics of problem solvers, and practices that galvanize institutions to better serve student populations. Moreover, we elucidated institutional practices that facilitate or hinder effective transition and learning. We also highlighted how this becomes particularly complicated at institutions with complex structures. Institutional leaders recognizing new patterns and nuances, having power to make change, creating systems and structures that better support a specific

55

population of students, understanding what expertise is necessary, and working with others to identify students who need individual assistance, all facilitate student success. Having identified facilitator behaviors, we now turn to explaining a comprehensive model that can guide educators and staff to advocate with and on behalf of SVSM.

Chapter 4

Advocacy Model

Student affairs professionals have endeavored to create a campus that is welcoming and affirming for all students through addressing multicultural issues in higher education (Pope, Reynolds, & Muller, 2004). In fact, multicultural competence is an essential component of student affairs practice as it is "a necessary prerequisite to effective, affirming, and ethical work in student affairs" (Pope & Reynolds, 1997, p. 270). Today, major professional organizations, such as ACPA —College Student Educators International, NASPA—Student Affairs Administrators in Higher Education, and the Council for the Advancement of Standards in Higher Education (CAS), unanimously emphasize the importance of multicultural competence and stress the use of advocacy as one of the key proficiencies to create truly multicultural campuses. However, little information is available to guide higher education administrators and student affairs professionals to effectively engage in advocacy work. Therefore, in this chapter, we focus on advocacy specific to the SVSM population. First, we discuss multicultural competence in student affairs and why advocacy is needed on behalf of SVSM. Then, we introduce the American Counseling Association (ACA) Advocacy Competencies (Lewis et al., 2002) to illustrate a variety of advocacy actions that student affairs professionals, higher education administrators, faculty, and staff can engage in to facilitate SVSM's successful integration and development in college.

MULTICULTURAL COMPETENCE FOR SERVING SVSM

One of the important missions of student affairs professionals is to support student development and create programs and services that enhance the potential for success in college. As the student population becomes more diverse, student affairs professionals, higher education administrators, faculty, and staff must develop effective strategies to foster student development within a context of increased diversity. To this end, Pope et al. (2004) identified developing multicultural competence as one of the seven core professional competencies for student affairs professionals. Pope et al. described multicultural competence as "*multicultural awareness, knowledge, and skills,* [that] entails the awareness of one's assumptions, biases, and values; an understanding of the worldview of others; information about various cultural groups; and developing appropriate intervention strategies and techniques" (p. 9; italics in original).

The original emphasis on multicultural competence focused primarily on working with racial and ethnic minority groups. Yet, the use of this competency is also imperative in working with other unique groups of students on today's campuses, including SVSM. Indeed, SVSM is a distinct cultural group whose numbers are rapidly increasing on many campuses. As described in Chapter 2, SVSM bring aspects of a unique military culture to higher education so that the clash of cultures between the military and higher education creates a variety of difficulties in their transition to college life. As we will detail in Chapter 6, the military experiences of SVSM have a significant influence on their cognitive development as well as identity development. Given the unique cultural backgrounds and experiences that SVSM bring to the college environment, we strongly believe that it is crucial for higher education administrators and student affairs professionals to utilize multicultural competence to work effectively with SVSM.

ADVOCACY

In higher education, advocacy is endorsed as an essential social justice strategy for facilitating a change process to create multicultural organizations on campus (Pope et al., 2004). Although some higher education professionals tend to work with students at an individual level, "if the campus system creates barriers (internal or external) that interfere with students' ability to succeed, then it seems appropriate to advocate for change within the system" (Pope et al., 2004, p. 93). Indeed, the need to identify systemic barriers and to advocate for removing those obstacles is included in the Equity, Diversity, and Inclusion (EDI) competency set forth by the ACPA and the NASPA (2010) as follows:

- Identify systemic barriers to equality and inclusiveness, and then advocate for and implement means of dismantling them;
- Apply advocacy skills to assist in the development of a more multiculturally sensitive institution and profession.

(p. 11)

Although advocacy is strongly encouraged as a part of professional competencies within the field, the actual ability of higher education administrators and student affairs professionals to successfully implement advocacy is unclear. First of all, there is a significant lack of literature in the field to guide effective advocacy work. Moreover, the few studies that exist on advocacy reveal that student affairs professionals actively resist engaging in system advocacy due to a variety of negative consequences resulting from their involvement in the advocacy action. For instance, Harrison (2010) found that student affairs professionals often experienced a conflict between maintaining their allegiances to students and their loyalties to upper-level administrators when they attempted to advocate for change. Similarly, Deanna (2001) found that student affairs professionals described advocacy as serving as "a voice for students" (p. 230) and believed in its importance, but they were also concerned if their engagement in advocacy could create potential threats to their professional careers. Furthermore, in a study of student affairs professionals' compliance with the ACPA's ethical principles and standards, Busher (1996) reported that student affairs professionals,

> felt that they had no power to override the directives of the person in authority, even if they believed the directives to be unethical. They perceived that it was useless to confront the authority about the unethical nature of the directives and feared possible consequences of doing so.
>
> (p. 122)

Given the importance of advocacy work, a lack of literature on advocacy, and significant difficulties in implementing successful advocacy, it was necessary for us to go beyond the field of higher education to search for literature that offers advocacy strategies needed for higher education administrators and student affairs professionals to create a multicultural campus. Therefore, in the next section, we describe the ACA Advocacy Competencies (Lewis et al., 2002). Though developed primarily for counselors, we believe that this framework offers useful structures for higher education administrators and student affairs professionals who are also called to serve as advocates for SVSM. The ACA Advocacy Competency model provides a useful guide for educators and administrators to decide what types of advocacy interventions are most effective, what conditions require which forms of advocacy methods, and what abilities, knowledge, and strategies are necessary to achieve advocacy to develop an ideal learning environment for students from diverse backgrounds (Arminio & Grabosky, 2013).

THE ACA ADVOCACY COMPETENCIES

The ACA Advocacy Competencies (Lewis et al., 2002) were created in a response to an increasing need for counselors to take on an advocacy role to effectively

59

address systemic and unjust conditions fundamental to clients' problems (Ratts, Toporek, & Lewis, 2010). Toporek and Liu (2001) defined advocacy as "action taken by counseling professionals to facilitate removal of external and institutional barriers to clients' well-being" (p. 387). There are two goals of advocacy: (a) to increase a client's sense of personal power and (b) to foster environmental changes that reflect greater responsiveness to a client's personal needs (Lewis, Lewis, Daniels, & D'Andrea, 1998). To achieve these goals, advocacy competence is defined as "the ability, understanding, and knowledge to carry out advocacy ethically and effectively" (Toporek, Lewis, & Crethar, 2009, p. 262). Consistent with these definitions and goals, the ACA advocacy competencies provide a much needed framework and specific guidance for counselors to incorporate advocacy in their professional practice.

The ACA Advocacy Competencies (Figure 4.1) are organized around the two interconnecting advocacy dimensions of Levels of Interventions and Extent of Client's Involvement (Ratts et al., 2010). Therefore, the model contains three ecological levels of advocacy intervention of a client: client/student, school/community, and public arena. Then, each of these advocacy levels is separated into two domains with regards to the degree of the client's involvement, whether advocacy work is *acting with* or *acting on behalf of* a client/student. Consequently, the model consists of six different areas of advocacy: (a) client/student empowerment; (b) client/student advocacy; (c) community collaboration; (d) systems advocacy; (e) public information; and (f) social/political advocacy. Below, we describe the advocacy model with examples from our study. For the purpose of this book, "higher education administrators and student affairs professionals" and "SVSM" are used to replace "counselor" and "client" to make it more appropriate for work with the SVSM population in higher education.

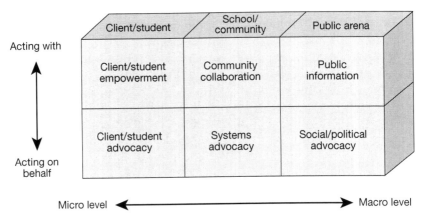

Figure 4.1 American Counseling Association Advocacy Competencies

Source: Lewis, Arnold, House, & Toporek, 2002 by the American Counseling Association. Reprinted with permission. No further reproduction authorized without permission from the American Counseling Association.

Student Level

In this level of advocacy, interventions take place at the micro level, focusing on the individual student. The advocacy interventions used in this level are *student empowerment* and *student advocacy*. Table 4.1 shows the list of SVSM advocacy competencies needed to successfully carry out each of the interventions in the Student Level.

In *student empowerment*, higher education administrators and student affairs professionals work directly with SVSM to help them create empowerment strategies. Since a majority of student affairs professionals provide direct interventions (e.g., advising, consulting, and mentoring), there are ample opportunities to engage in SVSM advocacy from the student empowerment domain. For instance, the following comments by Jason, a counseling center director at CC, illustrate the process of student empowerment in a career counseling session.

One of the key things was how to put his [military] service records into his resume, which is something that he hadn't done on his own. A counselor was

Table 4.1 SVSM Advocacy Competencies for Student Level

Advocacy Domain	Student Empowerment *Acting with*	Student Advocacy *Acting on behalf*
Advocacy Competencies	1. Identify strengths and resources of SVSM	1. Negotiate relevant services and education systems on behalf of SVSM
	2. Identify the social, political, economic, and cultural factors that affect SVSM	2. Help SVSM gain access to needed resources
	3. Recognize the signs indicating that SVSM's behaviors and concerns reflect responses to systemic problems	3. Identify barriers to the well-being of SVSM individuals and groups
	4. At an appropriate development level, help SVSM identify the external barriers that affect his or her development.	4. Develop initial plan of action for confronting these barriers
	5. Train SVSM in self-advocacy skills	5. Identify potential allies for confronting the barriers
	6. Help SVSM develop self-advocacy action plans.	6. Carry out the plan of action
	7. Assist SVSM in carrying out action plans	

Note: Modified from Lewis et al. 2002

working with him to adapt it. A lot of service men and women don't fully look at all the experience that they got through their time in [the military] and document that well on a resume, because they just look at "Oh yeah. I was in the military for 4, 6, 8, 10 years." "What did you do? What skills did you get?" Even trainings that they went through, they don't even list on their resumes. We help tease them out with them, so that we are fully showing what they have accomplished.

Here, Jason helped the SVSM to identify the strengths he brings to his career development and to effectively present his military training and duties to potential civilian employers. Given the ongoing job discrimination faced by many veterans, empowering SVSM by implementing civilian world career development strategies is a critical advocacy action in which student affairs professionals, higher education administrators, faculty, and staff can engage.

To successfully provide student empowerment interventions, it is crucial for higher education administrators and student affairs professionals to understand the influence of social, cultural, political, and economic issues of the college experience on SVSM. To this end, higher education administrators and student affairs professionals must be able to identify contextual factors (i.e., military training and culture) that affect SVSM's lives and prompt them to understand their own experience in college. Andrew, director of campus veterans services at CC, empowered SVSM by connecting military training and culture to SVSM experience in college as he intervened concerning the "aggressive" behaviors of SVSM.

Maybe their [SVSM] loans didn't disperse or whatever the case might be. Usually it's where they're aggressive. That's where I will step in and take that threat away from the work studies, and I sit down with that student. I don't like to call it PTSD because it may not be. I tell them my story. "You know I've been through that [military]. I don't have a lot of patience. Do I blame it on the military? Yes! Because I was trained that way: I was told to do it, so I would do it."

Andrew clearly understands the effect of military culture on the interpersonal behavior of SVSM as well as society's stereotypes and ignorance that SVSM may experience on a college campus. Thus, Andrew used his military cultural knowledge to validate SVSM's experiences and helped them understand how cultural issues affect their experiences in college. In addition, Andrew recognized the signs of cultural insensitivity and taught SVSM culturally appropriate ways to navigate interactions with other members of the campus community.

They [SVSM] are frustrated with an instructor because they're being called out as a veteran. I advise the students to talk with the instructor. Sit down with them first. Don't embarrass them in class. Don't call them out in class, like "Hey wait a minute here. I was doing what I was told to do whatever it might be [in the military]." But, you talk with the instructor privately. Maybe they didn't realize they said something that offended you. If it doesn't fix it, then we'll take it to the dean and let the dean know. "Hey we're seeing this from this instructor."

As evidenced in Andrew's advising, SVSM received support as well as an opportunity to learn appropriate ways to advocate for themselves in the context of a college environment. Therefore, student empowerment interventions serve as the foundation for SVSM self-advocacy.

When SVSM lack access to needed services, educators may decide to respond by advocating *on behalf of* SVSM. This form of advocacy intervention is called *student advocacy*. Here, higher education administrators and student affairs professionals negotiate education systems in support of SVSM to help them gain access to necessary resources. The following story by Jason, the counseling center director at CC, is a good example of student advocacy.

> I had a situation where a student got all F's in a term when she was called into active duty, but that got very tricky in terms of exactly what has happened. I really had to work closely with [the situation]. I actually went to our central coordinator for veterans affairs. In my review of the situation, I felt that we, as an institution, had not treated this person fairly, so I worked with the coordinator for veterans affairs, and we were able to back track and change her record to one that reflected that she went into the service and it did not reflect negatively on her.

Consistent with the concept of student advocacy described in the model, Jason recognized the institution's unfairness that hindered the SVSM's success in college. Therefore, he identified the veterans affairs coordinator as an ally and successfully confronted specific barriers in the institutional system. In other words, he effectively executed student advocacy by developing strategies to remove contextual barriers on behalf of SVSM.

Another example of student advocacy can be seen in the following statements by Stan, a director of veterans services at a large RI. He advocated on behalf of SVSM to provide them better access to mental health services in the following ways:

> I'm hitting the medical community, the counseling community, and the disability services community, and I worked with their directors. Stigma and mental health is a problem. [Veterans] who need counseling don't always walk into the building because it says "Counseling" on the front door. Our

counseling center was very flexible to sending someone down [to our office]. So, one counselor from our counseling center on campus is at our department once a week for scheduling for a block of time. She did her Ph.D. internships at VA medical centers on the PTSD wards. So she is just the right person to be coming over here.

On behalf of SVSM, Stan negotiated with directors of various offices that deal with SVSM mental health issues and helped SVSM gain access to desirable counseling services. In this process, he identified stigma as one of the major barriers and developed a strong alliance with the counseling center for confronting the obstacles. As a result, he successfully carried out the plan of advocacy action.

School/Community Level

In this level, advocacy is focused on systemic and organizational changes. This level of advocacy includes *community collaboration* and *systems advocacy*. Table 4.2 provides the list of advocacy competencies specific to SVSM for each domain.

To begin the school/community level of intervention, higher education administrators and student affairs professionals need to identify contextual barriers that impinge on the development of SVSM in college. An example is seen in the following statements by Glen, the vice president of student affairs at RI, which had gone through a significant transformation to provide effective services for SVSM:

> As a student affairs professional I saw it as my job to make sure these students had a positive experience, being able to connect with people in a community and could really become part of us as an institution so that we could invest in their success. I knew that if I could get them connected with other students that knew how to do this and with professionals who could help them through, we had a very good chance of making them successful. As a student affairs professional, it was my job to make sure that these students got the services and programs they needed to be successful. It was clear to me that the university was *not* doing it and we needed to do a better job.

Consistent with the first competency listed in the school/community level advocacy, Glen clearly recognized problems within the university system that created barriers to SVSM's success. Therefore, systemic change was needed to help SVSM to integrate into the college campus.

To implement *community collaboration* to advocate *with* SVSM, higher education administrators and student affairs professionals serve as allies or facilitators for SVSM individuals and groups to resolve systemic barriers that SVSM face on

Table 4.2 SVSM Advocacy Competencies for School/Community Level

	Community Collaboration *Acting with*	Systems Advocacy *Acting on behalf*
Advocacy Competencies	1. Identify environmental factors that impinge upon SVSM development	1. Identify environmental factors that impinge on SVSM development
	2. Alert SVSM community or group with common concerns related to the issue	2. Provide and interpret data to show the urgency for change
	3. Develop alliances with groups working for change	3. In collaboration with other stakeholders, develop a vision to guide change
	4. Use effective listening skills to gain understanding of the group's goals	4. Analyze the sources of political power and social influence within the university system
	5. Identify the strengths and resources that the group members bring to the process of systemic change	5. Develop a step-by-step plan for implementing the change process
	6. Communicate recognition of and respect for these strengths and resources	6. Develop a plan for dealing with probable responses to change
	7. Identify and offer the skills that higher education administrators & student affairs professionals can bring to the collaboration	7. Recognize and deal with resistance
	8. Assess the effect of higher education administrators' & student affairs professionals' interaction with the community	8. Assess the effect of higher education administrators' & student affairs professionals' advocacy efforts on the system and constituents

Note: Modified from Lewis, Arnold, House, & Toporek (2002)

campus. Glen reflected on how his university began collaborating with a SVSM advocacy group in his school:

The president gave a speech in September before the university senate. Two young men stood up and asked the president, why it was that our university did such a poor job of supporting veterans and why he did not support the student veterans that were here. The president said "Of course, I support the services for veterans that are here." The student said, "You provide no services, no support and it is hard for us to survive without the kinds of services we think are necessary to move forward." I had already pulled together some people for a meeting to begin to discuss some issues [impacting student veterans] that I became aware of. At the end of the speech the president came up to me and said "Look into this and see what's going on."

As indicated in the competency model, the issues raised by SVSM at this university were taken seriously and they became a departure point of *community collaboration*. Michael, one of the students who confronted the president, remembered this encounter with a sense of excitement:

> The president said he's really going to look into it! A week later, he created a veterans' advisory board and he invited us there. I was forthright with the president about a lot of issues. We gave advice about certain programs.

Michael's statements clearly reflect the university's effort to understand the experience of SVSM on campus and their advocacy goals. This action by the university was critical as identified in the school/community level of advocacy, which recommends the use of effective listening skills to understand the goals of the student group.

Another competency that higher education administrators and student affairs professionals need to demonstrate is the use of their expertise to facilitate community collaboration. Given their training and experience in higher education, these professionals possess critical knowledge and skills to understand organizations, politics, and cultures within the university system. Their interpersonal network and communication skills are also useful for the development of community collaboration. For instance, Glen employed his extensive knowledge and experience in higher education and leadership in the following ways:

> I put together an advisory council from across the university who were interested in veterans' services, and by across the university I mean across all three campuses of the university, including a number of people from other areas outside the university directly but that had an interest in it, such as people that were working in the state and people that were retired and had an interest in military things.

Glen used his professional power and expertise to make the university community aware of SVSM concerns and to build alliances with organizations that share common goals. Furthermore, Glen also utilized his professional network to locate a variety of resources on campus.

What I found interesting was how many people were already doing something connected with veterans' services on our campus. There are actually a lot of different people contributing in some ways. So, we pulled together resources and made commitments from experts that already existed here [on campus].

As seen in his comments, by collaborating with a variety of stakeholders on campus, Glen assisted SVSM advocacy by crafting approaches for addressing the lack of a unified support system for SVSM. Through these actions, Glen *acted with* the SVSM advocacy group to assist their mission to develop better services and programs on campus. Indeed, the success of community collaboration is clearly evident by Michele's comments.

Now, they have a veterans service director at every campus, veterans' orientations, veteran dinners, and a lot of different events. There are veteran student groups on every campus: there's a veterans services office at the main campus and veterans' lounge on other campuses. These are all different things that we advocated for. It has made a substantial difference.

Systems Advocacy

Another way to respond to systemic barriers is *systems advocacy*, in which higher education administrators and student affairs professionals advocate *on behalf of* SVSM to develop strategies for systemic change within the university. In this advocacy domain, higher education administrators and student affairs professionals become leaders, providing vision, conducting system analysis, collaborating with other stakeholders, and offering strong data to effectively change the system that contributes to the creation of many of the problems that SVSM encounter. For instance, Stan, a director of veterans services at RI, implemented *systems advocacy* to ease SVSM's transition to college in the following ways:

We've heard of frustrations where veterans go into an office and they're dealing with the person at the front desk and the person at the front desk is generally a work–study student, as opposed to somebody who can actually do something. So we created a network across the university with any office on campus that touches a student. That was the criteria. If an office touches a student, then they're going to touch a veteran as well. So we established these really wonderful points of contact, some at the vice president and associate vice president level; many at the dean and assistant or associate dean level, and some at the executive director and director level. So we are able to receive an issue from a veteran and in very short order send out an email or make a phone call to one of these people who has the authority to make a decision.

Here, to resolve inter-departmental problems that hinder SVSM's transition to college, Stan developed a clear vision by setting a "criteria" for the campus-wide network to effectively assist the development of SVSM in college. He successfully collaborated with the upper management level of professionals who have power to influence outcomes within the university's administrative system. His action clearly shows his understanding of the university's political process and how to work within the system. This knowledge is essential for successfully implementing systems advocacy.

Another important factor for systems advocacy is to provide strong evidence to support the need for change. To this end, higher education administrators and student affairs professionals can utilize their training in research, statistics, and assessment to collect information to support their arguments for change as well as to document the negative effects resulting from existing university procedures. For instance, Glen explained his effort to change information asked on admission applications to track SVSM at RI:

> We began tracking the graduation rates of our veteran students. I wanted to know if the resources we're putting in work and if they don't, [I want to know] where the gaps are. [I want to know] whether or not they're making adequate academic progress. If they aren't, we can track them down and figure out why they aren't. We began to collect the data. I know if I have the data, I can begin analyzing where we're successful. Without the data, I can't.

As suggested in the advocacy model, Glen gathered data to provide strong evidence of the efficacy of new programs that his leadership implemented. Furthermore, by providing financial analysis to show the university's benefits of an increased SVSM enrollment, Glen successfully gained significant support from powerful stakeholders in the university.

> We had a lot of support from the vice president of enrollment management and from the vice president of budget and planning. Both of them saw veterans as a good opportunity for us to attract high caliber people that were highly motivated, but that also had a secure source of income that would support them while they were in school.

By showing the interrelationships among the SVSM community, enrollment, graduation rates, and the university's financial revenue, Glen made a successful argument that a system change can indeed create more benefits not only for SVSM but also for many departments within the university. In fact, such comprehensive analysis of relationships among various parts of the system is critical for developing a systematic plan for change (Lopez-Baez & Paylo, 2009). In the end, Glen was able to obtain the full support of the president of the university to institute changes in the university.

We issued a report with various recommendations and we recommended to the president that we proceed with doing all these things. He said, "Go forward and do everything." We began the process of putting together a program in veteran services. I got a position as director of veteran services. There was a broken down old house and I arranged to have the house fixed up with resources I have in student affairs.

Through using a variety of actions also listed in the competency model, Glen effectively executed systems advocacy and provided much needed service and programs to the SVSM community in the university.

Public Arena Level

The public arena level of advocacy addresses SVSM issues at the macro level, aiming at the general public and society as a whole. This level of advocacy includes *public information* and *social/political advocacy*: The accompanying competencies targeting SVSM advocacy are listed in Table 4.3.

Through *public information*, higher education administrators, student affairs professionals, faculty, and staff, SVSM groups, and the community work together to increase the public's awareness about external barriers affecting the experience of the SVSM population. For instance, organizing campaigns or demonstrations is a great way to bring the public's attention to SVSM issues and to communicate the urgency for change to a wider audience. The central task in this advocacy is the development of communication strategies on a large scale through the use of various media. Jeremy, president of a SVSM group, described the following strategies that they used to conduct *public information* advocacy:

> We wanted to have a debate focusing on veterans' issues. I moderated it, and I was up in the front. There was me and this guy who owned a political talk show in the city, so we had him involved. We focused every question on Iraq and Afghanistan veteran issues. That was our stage. We were like, "Why doesn't the university have this program?" or "Why doesn't the school have this program?" We were like, "This is what we need . . . Bam, Bam, Bam!" We were all quoted in papers [the] next day.

Michael, another student leader of a SVSM group, also talked about the effective use of media as his strategy for advocacy. He described what happened in an anti-war rally at his university:

> A picture with the three policemen and me holding that flag got put up in a [news] paper. So I did the same thing that Martin Luther King [Jr.] did, basically expanded the scope and influence. So I had other people outside the college community looking at this [picture].

69

Table 4.3 SVSM Advocacy Competencies for Public Arena Level

Advocacy Domain	Public information *Acting with*	Social/Political Advocacy *Acting on behalf*
Advocacy Competencies	1. Recognize the impact of external barriers to healthy development	1. Distinguish those problems that can best be resolved through social/political action
	2. Identify environmental factors that are protective of healthy development	2. Identify the appropriate mechanisms and avenues for addressing these problems
	3. Prepare written and multi-media materials that provide clear explanations of the role of specific environmental factors in human development	3. Seek out and join with potential allies
	4. Communicate information in ways that are ethical and appropriate for the target population	4. Support existing alliances for change
	5. Disseminate information through a variety of media	5. With allies, prepare convincing data and rationales for change
	6. Identify and collaborate with other professionals who are involved in disseminating public information	6. With allies, lobby legislators and other policy makers
	7. Assess the influence of public information efforts undertaken by the student affairs professional	7. Maintain open dialogue with SVSM communities and students to ensure that the social/political advocacy is consistent with the initial goals

Note: Modified from Lewis, Arnold, House, & Toporek (2002)

As described in the model, Jeremy and Michael successfully disseminated information through a variety of media outlets. In a similar way, advocates can use television, print media, and the Internet as powerful tools to inform the public about systemic issues that negatively affect SVSM's success in college. To this end, higher education administrators and student affairs professionals can also collaborate with other professionals to educate the larger public about SVSM issues. For instance, Stan, the director of campus veterans services at RI, teamed up with other professionals: "We just finished and it's in the editing process right now. We wrote a guide from military to college. Our part is on setting up veterans' services on campus." In fact, higher education administrators and student affairs professionals have a unique opportunity to provide real accounts of SVSM experience on today's campuses. Thus, writing articles in both print and electronic media is not only effective in raising the public's awareness but also serves as a vehicle for influencing policy makers and challenging politicians to endorse legislation that upholds services to SVSM in college.

Social/political advocacy is chosen when administrators need to advocate at a policy and legislative level to resolve environmental constraints that negatively affect SVSM. This type of advocacy is appropriate when higher education administrators and student affairs professionals recognize that public policy itself is causing difficulties in SVSM's college development. Therefore, they decide to act *on behalf of* SVSM to work toward changes in public policy that would address problems experienced by SVSM. The following is a good example of social/political advocacy by Glen, the VP at RI, who recognized a lack of national statistics on SVSM:

> The issue that became clear to us was that the federal government appears to be putting a lot of money into veterans affairs, and veterans services, and veterans education. [But] There was no national data that we were able to find . . . So you put hundreds of billions of dollars into these programs, and we can't tell you whether or not those programs are successful!

To address this national-level problem affecting SVSM and higher education, Glen conducted *political advocacy* as follows:

> I put forward a proposal to develop a research center on veterans' services. We began lobbying in Washington, D.C. We met with veterans at the head of educational programs for higher education in the veterans affairs office.

As suggested in the model, Glen as well as other higher education administrators whom we interviewed, had lobbied local, state, and federal legislators and policy makers to communicate the need to improve SVSM's experience and retention in higher education. In organizing a lobbying effort, Lee and Rodgers (2009) emphasized two crucial issues for the advocates: (a) to "present with a united front and speak with one clear voice on the issue" (p. 87); and (b) to provide "convincing data and a strong rationale for change" (p. 87). Also, Lee and Rodgers (2009) stressed strong leadership, clear strategic visions, effective research skills, and courage as the critical characteristics for social and political advocates and listed the six essential factors for success: (a) acting with purpose; (b) being ethical; (c) maintaining open communication among stakeholders; (d) visible media efforts; (e) strategic thinking; and (f) collaboration. Successful advocacy at this level can make a significant impact in the lives of SVSM as Michael described his group's victory of social/political advocacy:

> We wanted universities and colleges in this state to have websites that make their resources transparent for military veteran students, so that you can evaluate what university or college has the best qualities for you. So, I ended up working with an assemblyman who was the military veteran affairs committee chair and a senator who is the military veterans' affairs committee chair in this state. We actually got a bill passed for that and now all the universities and colleges in this state have a website or web link that makes the resources transparent.

Through successful social/political advocacy, Michael created important resources available for all veterans who are seeking higher education opportunities in his state.

Challenging systemic barriers to promote social justice among students is a significant professional endeavor. However, it is also very important to be aware of potential risks of becoming involved in public arena advocacy. Public action against social inequalities may create personal and professional difficulties, such as harassment in the workplace, a reputation as a "troublemaker," disciplinary actions, or limited career advancement opportunities (Lee & Rodgers, 2009). To this end, Lee and Rodgers (2009) recommended thoughtful examination and self-exploration upon engaging in social/political advocacy.

> Social/political advocates must consider such risks as part of the process of promoting a just society. They must reach a point in their own personal and professional lives where they believe that the benefit to the common good from their social/political advocacy is well worth the risks.
>
> (p. 287)

We strongly believe in the importance of social/political advocacy work in higher education to promote and create equality and social justice among all students. Nonetheless, we also agree with Lee and Rodgers that it is "personal courage" (p. 287) that drives professionals to advocate at the public arena level.

CONCLUSION

We recommend the use of the ACA advocacy competencies as a guide to create a multicultural environment for SVSM to integrate into their college campus. As described in this chapter, the ACA advocacy model requires higher education administrators and student affairs professionals to maximize multi-cultural competencies, to work closely with the student community, to initiate interdisciplinary collaboration, to confront systemic barriers, and to determine the course for advocacy goals (Toporek et al., 2009). Also, this framework provides guidance on how to consider and engage in several levels of advocacy. The multiple levels of advocacy described in this model are especially helpful for higher education administrators and student affairs professionals who represent a wide range of training and specialties (Arminio & Grabosky, 2013). For instance, mid-level administrators can utilize competencies for the school/community level as they work closely with university systems and organizations, whereas student affairs professionals who work directly with students can learn from the student/client level of advocacy (Arminio & Grabosky, 2013). Leadership, including deans, vice presidents, chancellors, and presidents, should utilize their professional power and networks in the systems as well as public arena levels of advocacy. This can influence stakeholders of the university as well as social and political figures who serve the public. Furthermore, their leadership in advocacy is fundamental to developing a professional environment that fosters and demonstrates advocacy across the institution. In all respects, this model offers a variety of competencies and possibilities for the effective implementation of SVSM advocacy work on college campuses.

Utilizing the advocacy model in this chapter can lead institutions to establish best practices in serving SVSM. Such practices are recognized as those most likely to empower SVSM to reach their learning potential. We address best practices next.

Chapter 5

Best Practices for Increasing Student Success

To initiate our discussion on best practices, we begin with a scenario.

Chris serves as an academic advisor at a large public doctoral-degree-granting institution and receives an email from a new student, Jamie, who is interested in a particular academic program but is having trouble navigating the registration systems. Jamie is a former Marine, works part-time, and is trying to determine an appropriate career path. Due to continual problems with enrolling in classes and after several email and phone exchanges, the two decide it would be best to meet in person. In Chris's office Jamie enrolls in two courses, but is unaware of any of the orientation opportunities the institution offers student veterans. Jamie has visited the veterans services office on campus, but only to inquire about GI Bill benefits. Toward the end of the semester Jamie makes a return visit to Chris in desperation over poor grades. Jamie's instructors note that papers lack depth, seem hurried, and need to be proofread more carefully. Wanting clarification, Jamie asks what the feedback means. How might Chris proceed? What institutional and unit best practices relate to this scenario?

In this chapter we define good and best practices. We also describe their usefulness, but expose cautions in relying too heavily on best practices. We follow with a discussion connecting best practices to problem solving. We provide recognized practices that support SVSM as they transition into, through, and graduate from higher education institutions. We offer institutional best practices, then list recommended practices of various functional areas, offices, and services across higher education. We end by reconnecting with the opening scenario. This chapter dovetails with topics in Chapters 3 and 4, but here we focus on concrete practices and services offered by specific offices, units, or departments. We start with institutional practices and then turn to the areas of veterans services, enrollment management (including registration, financial aid, and admissions), academic advising, counseling, health services, disability services, career services, residence life, campus programs and student union management, diverse student population resource centers, and assessment.

LITERATURE ABOUT GOOD AND BEST PRACTICES

Literature on good practices in higher education is common. For example, Chickering and Gamson (1987) described good practices in undergraduate education as encompassing the following:

1. contact between students and faculty
2. reciprocity and cooperation among students
3. active learning
4. prompt feedback
5. substantial time on task
6. high expectations, and
7. promotion of diverse talents and ways of learning.

(p. 4)

Though Chickering and Gamson felt that these practices individually manifest important gains, they stressed that their cumulative effect is particularly beneficial. Combined, these good practices in higher education "employ six powerful forces." They are:

- activity
- expectations
- cooperation
- interaction
- diversity, and
- responsibility.

(p. 7)

Another example, in the literature of descriptors of good practice, is *Good Practice in Student Affairs* (1999). Here, Blimling, Whitt, and Associates stressed that educators should follow good practice principles in response to forces advocating for change in higher education including increased calls for accountability and distance education options. Meant to be flexible for use by "varied educational institutions with diverse groups of students and campus climates" (p. 14), these principles of good practice are:

- engaging students in active learning
- prompting students to develop coherent values and ethical standards
- communicating and setting high expectations for students
- employing systematic assessment methods to improve student learning and institutional performance
- prioritizing the use of resources to accomplish institutions' missions and goals
- marshaling partnerships that stimulate student learning, and
- ensuring supportive and inclusive environments.

Both Blimling et al. (1999) and Chickering and Gamson (1987) stressed active learning, setting high expectations, and learning in collaboration with others.

Baum and Stoller (2014) defined a best practice as "any process, program, or intervention developed by an external entity espoused as an ideal solution to be applied towards a similar scenario". Considering best practices avoids a singular focus, emphasizes commonalities among differing views, offers succinct information that can be easily understood, and "forms principles that can be applied in multiple situations" (Blimling et al., 1999, p. 14).

However, Baum and Stoller (2014) argued that solely looking to external agencies for best practices may not be advantageous for organizations. They asserted that the only kind of problems that can be addressed by best practices are those that are well defined, have objectively right or wrong solutions that are easily tried and abandoned, and have limited alternatives. More complex problems have no defined end points, are unique, and their solutions have unintended consequences, often creating more problems (McCormack, 2009; Weick, 2005). Best practices can inhibit imagination in that new information is organized into previously understood "categories, stereotypes, and schemas" (Weick, 2005, p. 432).

We caution readers that not all concerns facing SVSM are simple problems with identifiable solutions. We recognize that issues discussed in this book may never be solved permanently (e.g., Will the cultural incongruences of higher education and the U.S. military organizations ever subside? Will the world ever end its wars and the need for its young to interrupt their education to fight in them?). We also recognize that the contextual nuances of institutions, campuses, and students play a determining role in what practices should be implemented and how. Educators should not utilize a one-size-fits-all approach, but create and maintain programs and services that address the needs of individual SVSM on their particular campus (Reisser, 2011). We further recognize that good and best practices are those that are validated in the literature or created through consensus (such as the CAS Standards, 2012). In particular, we discuss specific practices that align with those advocated for by Chickering and Gamson (1987) and Blimling et al. (1999).

Institutional leaders are tasked with the responsibility of creating a campus climate conducive to learning and ultimately degree attainment. Units within the institution must ensure that they play a role in contributing to an engaging institutional environment. In particular to SVSM, it is crucial that there are institutional and unit initiatives that integrate SVSM as members of the campus community. We identify these initiatives below.

INSTITUTIONAL BEST PRACTICES

Still a predominantly human-dependent enterprise, higher education institutions must pay careful attention to the training and expertise of their employees.

Offering continual training, education, and development for faculty, staff, and administrators to be equipped to work with all students is an essential practice. At Virginia Commonwealth University a "Green Zone" program was created. This program is similar to Safe Zone programs for LGBT students in which educators who attend specialized training display a "Green Zone" sticker indicating that they are interested, willing, and have been trained to work with SVSM (Nichols-Casebolt, 2012). According to Nichols-Casebolt, a SVSM exclaimed, "Even if I don't need any assistance, it makes me feel good to see the Green Zone sticker on someone's door" (p. 29).

Because of the cultural differences between the military and academia, as described in Chapter 2, establishing trust between campus employees and SVSM is vital. This occurs through clear, open, and continuous communication (Francis & Kraus, 2012). Moreover, institutions need to be sure that there are opportunities that "blur the boundaries between veteran and non-veteran communities and help to build cross-cultural relationships that benefit all groups" (Francis & Kraus, 2012, p. 14). These cross-cultural relationships include creating learning partnerships where mentors allow students to direct their learning, but with close advising (Baxter Magolda, 2011). An example would be a thesis or research project, or service-learning initiative.

Training to recognize potential learning difficulties due to wounds of war is paramount. Faculty and staff must be aware of the limitations such conditions impose and make appropriate classroom accommodations (ACE, 2010a, 2010b). Training should also highlight the significant influence that the VA and the military still has on the lives of SVSM, such as difficulties in scheduling VA appointment and weekend military duties. Providing greater flexibility for these students to make up missed assignments will help to create a more veteran supportive campus (Kognito Interactive, 2013).

One way to advocate for more funding for SVSM is to enroll in the Yellow Ribbon Program in which campuses agree with the VA to help fund SVSM tuition and fee expenses that exceed the highest public in-state undergraduate tuition rate in their state. Institutions can contribute an amount that the VA will match as long as it doesn't exceed 50% of the difference (U.S. Department of Veterans Affairs, 2012).

CAMPUS VETERANS SERVICES

Vacchi (2012) noted that SVSM often experience similar difficulties that other students experience, such as "lack of ability to navigate the systems of bureaucracy of a college campus" (p. 19). Moving back and forth between military and campus cultures is particularly difficult for National Guard and Reserve members who leave campus to deploy, attend training, and meet other service obligations. Responsibilities of campus veterans services include ensuring a welcoming campus environment for SVSM, supporting their success in college, and advocating for appropriate policies and procedures that accommodate their military obligations. The campus veterans services director is the point person for SVSM (Griffith & Gilbert, 2012) who guides, supports, and advocates for SVSM (Childress & Childress, 2011). The director ensures one-on-one support so that SVSM have "socializing agents" as suggested by Schlossberg (2011, p. 18).

The campus veterans services director must understand the military culture, including its structures and language as well as how the military backgrounds of SVSM affect their experience on campus. As stressed in Chapter 2, there is a unique rolodex of phrases embedded in the highly structured military environment. To assist SVSM, the director must have an ability to bridge the cultural gap between the military and higher education. The campus veterans services director might also provide a means of connecting the institution with families of SVSM through regular meetings and events with family members (DiRamio & Jarvis, 2011).

To create support networks and ensure effective services, it is important that campus veterans services has an advisory committee comprised of administrators, staff, and faculty representing disability services, admissions, counseling services, enrollment management, and campus programs and services (Military Family Research Institute at Purdue University and SVA, 2013). This too could increase resources and collaboration.

Veterans services should collect data on the SVSM population to understand the factors that affect student veteran engagement, retention, persistence, and degree attainment. Data analysis should include both short- and long-term goals for supporting SVSM as well as the impact that SVSM have on and off campus, including economic value to the institution and the community. In addition, data should be used to guide strategies for providing effective veteran support programs and to demonstrate return on investment for the institution.

Advocating for SVSM is another important mission for campus veterans services. Vacchi (2012) described entrance obstacles for SVSM within the same institution as: (a) inconsistent methods for assigning credit for military service; (b) little consistency for awarding course credits earned while in the military; and (c) differences in what credits count toward a degree. Veterans services should take the leadership to reduce such inconsistencies within the institution as well as across feeder institutions.

To assist in navigating the bureaucracy of a college campus and the VA, campus veterans services should create a formalized checklist for SVSM such as CC did with their Yellow Sheet. This checklist of procedures and particular offices to consult should be made available both online and in print for SVSM to easily access the resource (ACE, 2013a). Campus veterans services should ensure that special orientation programs are offered to connect incoming SVSM with those currently enrolled. Given the significant impact that loss of camaraderie has on the experience of SVMS on campus, it is critical for campus veterans services to recreate the familiar support that SVSM were accustomed to in the military. Mentor programs, SVSM panel discussions, and veteran-to-veteran tutoring programs can serve as avenues for creating new military camaraderie within the context of higher education (Lang, 2012). Campus veterans services should utilize the VA Work Study program to employ SVSM. Not only does this program offer financial assistance, but it also provides an opportunity for SVSM to play a role in creating an effective support program for SVSM (O'Neil, 2013). Both RI and CC had vibrant work–study SVSM programs.

Campuses throughout the country have reported significant success with increases in SVSM enrollment and retention after opening a veterans resource center (Dykman, 2013). This is essentially a one-stop shop for SVSM that fully integrates all facets of student veteran support services, state and federal veteran programs, and student veteran organizations in one location.

ENROLLMENT MANAGEMENT

In addition to serving on the veteran services advisory committee to assist in streamlining the admissions process for SVSM (University of Missouri Veteran Task Force, 2008), enrollment management should track applicants' acceptance and degree progress. This is imperative because the Integrated Postsecondary Education Data System (IPEDS) only tracks students on a first-time, full-time status, but not the interruptions common in the SVSM graduation cycle or prior military education. To this end, the admissions application should consist of a question asking an applicant's military service experience and duty status as well as if an applicant is a family member receiving benefits (Ohio University, 2013). Tracking SVSM is often a difficult practice for higher education institutions to implement because SVSM may not disclose that they are a veteran. To encourage SVSM to disclose their service, institutions could consider waiving the application fees or providing priority-class registration (ACE, 2013a).

Transcript review policies should be posted and clearly outlined. Transcripts must be reviewed fairly and completed in a timely manner prior to SVSM enrolling in classes. Also, academic advisors must be well-trained to evaluate transcripts for SVSM who have attended several different institutions (DiRamio & Jarvis, 2011). This will help to ensure that SVSM maximize their educational benefits (ACE, 2013b). In addition, priority registration should be given to students utilizing the GI Bill so that they can graduate within their allotted benefits time constraint. Withdrawal and re-admission policies should accommodate student members of the National Guard and Reservists who may be called to duty throughout a semester. Re-enrollment should be as seamless as possible.

79

Recruitment

To conduct effective SVSM recruitment, it is critical that admissions counselors collaborate with campus veterans services to establish recruitment strategies. Campus veterans services can assist admissions counselors to network with organizations that support veterans and offer more access to SVSM. Admissions counselors can also work directly with local and regional National Guard and Reserve units, Family Readiness Groups (command-sponsored organizations of volunteers that provide support for military members and their families), and Blue Star Mothers (a congressionally chartered organization that assists active duty military personnel and veterans).

Providing evidence of a veteran-friendly campus is essential to increase SVSM's enrollment on campus. Therefore, admissions counselors should demonstrate institutional support for SVSM by presenting statistics on the SVSM population as well as programs and services specific to SVSM. Several resources are available for institutions to collect data within the state. These include the American Fact Finder, the VA, and Defense Actuary, which stores data on age, gender, and location of SVSM (see Appendix).

Financial Aid

It is important to recognize that not all of the SVSM population will receive sufficient benefits to cover 100% of the cost of their education. Therefore, financial aid officers will need to advise these students about federal programs to help fund their education, especially if they are from outside of the state. To assist SVSM to obtain more funding, it is important for financial aid officers to be aware of a variety of institution and private funding sources.

ACADEMIC ADVISING

In advising SVSM, academic advisors might consider pointing out to SVSM who are transferring many credits, which degree programs could be completed more easily (Pellegrin, 2013). Advisors should consider the individual needs and strengths of SVSM and be aware of veteran-specific courses offered (DiRamio & Jarvis, 2011). Courses that encourage SVSM to write about, reflect upon, and make meaning of their military experience can be especially useful in connecting their military experiences to other coursework (DiRamio & Jarvis, 2011).

Wilson and Smith (2012) used the differentiation of life and working missions in their advising strategies with SVSM. They encouraged academic advisors to interact with SVSM about both the working mission (course enrollments, degree attainment) but also the core life mission (assumptions that ground the working mission and its relevancy to one's sense of purpose). For example, in the scenario

80

beginning this chapter, Jamie indicated to Chris that majoring in accounting is important because of the job prospects, salary, and other benefits that line of work would provide. However, Chris asks Jamie to explain how accounting relates to Jamie's course papers, which expose an interest in serving others in the non-public sector. Wilson and Smith (2012) urged academic advisors to allow SVSM to come to their own conclusions about what working mission best supports the life mission. Best practices in academic advising are those that "empower students not only to take control of their educational future but to meld their educational aspirations with their current position and understood life mission" (Wilson & Smith, 2012, p. 68). This requires that advisers view their work with SVSM through both a "transient lens" and a more "permanent lens" (p. 70). For example, an adviser would discuss how a course schedule (transient lens) relates to or detracts from the life mission (a more permanent lens). According to Wilson and Smith, SVSM "need to play an active role in college decision making" (p. 72).

COUNSELING

Counseling center staff must develop cultural competencies to understand and appreciate the influence of the military culture on the experience of SVSM in college (Black, Westwood, & Sorsdal, 2007; Bonar & Domenich, 2011). This is essential because: (a) the majority of college counselors are civilians with limited knowledge and experience with the military culture; and (b) it is impossible to fully understand the psychological experience of military service members without understanding the cultural values of the military (Christian et. al., 2009). Therefore, counseling center staff should obtain additional training on military culture, deployment cycles, reactions to combat trauma, and effective counseling interventions for veterans to adeptly understand the intersections of military life and college life in SVSM's psychological experience (Bonar & Domenich, 2011).

More specifically, counselors must recognize how military culture influences the stigma SVSM attach to those seeking mental health services. Whitley, Tschudi, and Giber (2013) listed several strategies to reduce the possible stigma SVSM hold about counseling and how to increase their utilization of counseling services. For instance, it is important for counseling centers to increase SVSM awareness and understanding of services available at college counseling centers because SVSM are accustomed to an environment where there is no privacy or confidentiality (Whitley et al., 2013). To make accessing counseling more comfortable for SVSM, counseling centers can change center signs to be less visible, to utilize language that is less associated with specific stigmas, and be flexible by offering counseling sessions at veterans' services offices when needed (Whitley et al., 2013). Also, a variety of choices, modalities, and services should be offered to provide multiple and comfortable support options for SVSM (ACE, 2013b; Whitley et al., 2013). For instance, counseling centers can create walk-in hours at the veterans services office, train and supervise SVSM leaders to facilitate informal interest groups, and offer formal therapy groups for SVSM, in addition to providing traditional individual counseling sessions (Whitley et al., 2013).

Because SVSM is often an invisible cultural group on campus, counseling centers should include a question in their intake assessment that asks about clients' military background and deployment experience (Bonar & Domenich, 2011). This simple question can improve the accurate identification of SVSM clients and counselors' awareness of cultural issues that SVSM clients bring to counseling sessions. When working with SVSM clients, it is critical for counselors to assess the military experience of clients to understand the cultural context of the client's presenting issues (Black et al., 2007). We recommend that counseling center staff obtain the following information during an initial assessment: (a) military service history, including motivation for joining, duration of service, branch, rank, duties, degree of combat experience, and reasons for separation; (b) overall experience in the military; (c) experience in college; (d) social network composition represented by civilians and veterans/military service members; (e) family military background; and (f) the level of personal significance of his or her identity as SVSM. This information can assist counseling center staff to conceptualize the SVSM client's cultural orientation and acculturation to the college environment and to develop culturally appropriate treatment plans in working with SVSM clients.

The majority of recommendations in the literature for counseling centers have been focused on providing effective service for combat-related psychological injuries such as Post-Traumatic Stress Disorder (PTSD) and Traumatic Brain Injury (TBI). Counseling centers should prepare themselves to provide assessment and treatment of PTSD (Rudd, Goulding, & Bryan, 2011; Zinger & Cohen, 2010). To this end, counseling center staff should be trained in the effective use of PTSD treatment approaches such as Exposure Therapy (ET), Cognitive Processing Therapy (CPT) and Eye Movement Desensitization and Reprocessing (EMDR), all of which are suggested as recommended treatment protocols for PTSD by the National Center for PTSD and the VA. Based on the alarming results of their national survey on the psychological symptoms and suicide risk of SVSM, Rudd et al. (2011) also stressed that counseling center staff be trained in suicide risk assessment unique to veterans with PTSD symptoms. Furthermore, ACE (2013a) recommended developing partnerships with the VA, Vet Centers, and local mental health professionals to provide various treatment options. Counseling centers should also develop extensive sources of referral for SVSM seeking mental health support (Zinger & Cohen, 2010).

Though war-related injuries are the reality affecting many SVSM, the focus in the current literature on the "wounded" or "disabled" portion of SVSM population has been criticized by Bonar and Domenici (2011), who argued that "the frequent depiction of military undergraduates as primarily disabled draws a misleading picture of this cultural group" (p. 208). In fact, the Center for Collegiate Mental Health (2013) reported that 67.4% of SVSM who received service at college counseling centers indicated that they had *not* experienced "traumatic or highly stressful experiences" (p. 9). The most common challenges among SVSM consistently reported in many studies are acculturation difficulties associated with transition from the military to campus. As Black et al. (2007) stated, "[t]ransition from the military into civilian life is inevitable for the majority of military members; successful transition is not" (p. 4). Therefore, counseling centers should play an essential role in facilitating *all* SVSM's successful adjustment to college (Zinger & Cohen, 2010) regardless of the existence of trauma, disability, and mental health problems.

To facilitate SVSM successful adjustment to college, counseling centers should actively provide more quality outreach programs to this population (Bonar & Domenici, 2011; Rudd et al., 2011). Furthermore, counseling centers must collaborate with the campus veterans services office and SVSM organizations as well as local military organizations (e.g., Vet Center, VA). Involving leaders in the SVSM community is critical to creating culturally appropriate programs and services for this population and to recreating the strong camaraderie and leadership essential to the military culture. To gain trust from SVSM whose culture is unique, it is crucial for civilian counselors to demonstrate their support and understanding by actively participating in SVSM programs, meeting SVSM on their turf. Casual conversations at these events can become opportunities for SVSM to informally assess the counselors' credibility and trustworthiness. These occasions are opportunities for building therapeutic alliances with the SVSM population.

Counselors can serve as cultural consultants to help equip SVSM with the knowledge and skills needed to succeed in college (Black et al., 2007). Furthermore, counselors should also serve as resources to create a multicultural campus environment. For example, counseling centers can train faculty and staff about military culture and SVSM's readjustment issues (Black et al., 2007) as well as war-related injuries such as PTSD and TBI. To effectively address systemic and organizational barriers underlying difficulties in SVSM adjusting to college, counselors should use the ACA Advocacy Model (Lewis et al., 2002) as a guide to advocacy work for creating a veteran-friendly campus (see Chapter 4 as well as Arminio & Grabosky, 2013, for more details).

HEALTH SERVICES

ACE (2013a) provided several ideas for best practices specific to health services. Health centers should consider including an intake assessment question of

"Are you currently or have you been a member of the United States Armed Forces?" to effectively identify students who need veteran-specific health care services. Also, health center staff should obtain and utilize the *Military Health-History Pocket Card for Clinicians,* which contains helpful information for understanding SVSM's medical issues, developing rapport with SVSM, and making sufficient and timely referrals to specialized care (U.S. Department of Veterans Health Administration, 2013). Displaying veteran-specific health services information on campus and in the local community is not only helpful for connecting SVSM with additional medical services but also for creating a welcoming atmosphere for SVSM. To meet the needs of an increasing SVSM population on campus and to obtain training, consultation, and make referrals when necessary, it is important for health centers to establish collaborative relationships with local providers specializing in veteran health care (e.g., the VA medical center, Vets Centers).

DISABILITY SERVICES

Professionals in disability services must understand a variety of unique factors that make it difficult for SVSM to self-identify and document their disabilities. Many of today's service-related disabilities are invisible (Shackelford, 2009); thus SVSM must voluntarily disclose their conditions to disability services. Yet, due to a strong emphasis on masculinity in the military, SVSM are often hesitant to self-identify disabilities acquired during their military service (Shackelford, 2009). Also, particular disabilities may take a longer period of time to develop or be diagnosed. Furthermore, government bureaucracy often causes delays in assessment, diagnoses, and documentation necessary for SVSM to obtain disability services (Shackelford, 2009). Unlike other students who have used disability services in secondary school, many SVSM with newly acquired disabilities are not aware of the existence of disability services and the reasonable accommodations process available to them (ACE, 2013a). Given the complexity of identifying and documenting SVSM with disabilities, it is critical for disability services to be proactive in reaching out to the SVSM population to communicate the purpose, availability, and benefits of disability services (ACE, 2013a). Moreover, staff in campus disability services should make sure that disability-related policies and procedures are made available to prospective and current SVSM that explain the role and specific responsibility of SVSM in the disability disclosure, documentation, and accommodation process (Shackelford, 2009). Given the anxiety that SVSM typically have about disability disclosure, disability service providers need to effectively communicate a high level of confidentiality when describing the procedures for release of disability information as well as how the information is stored safely (Burnett & Segoria,

2009). To reduce the stigma associated with having a documented disability, disability services should introduce the concept of *disability* from the perspective of the field of disability studies, in which disability is defined as "a sociopolitical construct created and perpetuated by an environment with barriers that exclude disabled people from access and participation" (Kraus & Rattray, 2013, p. 122). This model's strong emphasis on equal access, policy, and curricula with less focus on individuals' impairments, offers a familiar view for SVSM who were trained to fight for social justice (Kraus & Rattray, 2013). This sociopolitical construct repositions the cause of the problems to the environment instead of within the individual. In addition, disability service providers should become familiar with disability-related standards and procedures used in the military and VA (Shackelford, 2009) and help SVSM understand the differences between a VA disability rating and a disability under the Americans with Disabilities Act or Section 504 of the Rehabilitation Act (ACE, 2013a). To create SVSM-specific resources, disability service providers should be familiar with VA and other local health services available to SVSM (Shackelford, 2009).

Disability service providers should collaborate with campus veterans services on their campus to bridge the gap and create rapport with SVSM so that they become less reluctant to seek out disability services, connect with campuses resources, and utilize accommodations and support (Burnett & Segoria, 2009; Kraus & Rattray, 2013). Furthermore, disability services must see disability as a component of diversity and infuse this "broad concept of disability into campus practice" (Kraus & Rattray, 2013, p. 128). To this end, leaders of disability services should introduce and promote the use of Universal Design (Branker, 2009; Kraus & Rattray, 2013), defined as "the design of products and environments to be usable by all people, to the greatest extent possible, without the need for adaptation or specialized design" (Center for Universal Design, 1997). This inclusive approach to education is key to reducing stigma about disability and addressing the needs of all students.

In addition, disability services should take a leadership role in educating faculty and staff about the unique challenges that SVSM with disabilities bring to campus (ACE, 2013a; Shackelford, 2009). Oftentimes, a faculty member becomes the initial person who refers a SVSM with suspected disabilities to disability services. Therefore, it is important that professionals working in disability services prepare faculty to understand the common combat-related disability issues that SVSM may bring to their classrooms (Burnett & Segoria, 2009) as well as institutional, academic, and legal responsibilities that the institution has in working with SVSM with disabilities (Shackelford, 2009). In these trainings, disability services can instruct faculty to include a statement about information on campus veterans services as well as disability services on their course syllabi (ACE, 2013a). This effort can help increase SVSM's awareness and utilization of disability services on campus.

85

CAREER SERVICES

Career development concerns that SVSM bring to campus are largely an extension of transition issues from the military to civilian worlds of work. The need of SVSM for career transitional support on campus is mainly due to a lack of participation in transition assistance programs offered by the military (Simpson & Armstrong, 2009). Therefore, career counselors can assist SVSM in understanding what transitional assistance they missed and how they can obtain appropriate assistance. To help SVSM span this gap, career counselors can offer services specific to the needs of SVSM while developing partnerships with various veteran career development resources such as the U.S. Department of Defense/Department of Labor Transition Assistance Program (TAP) and American Corporate Partners (ACP).

According to Simpson and Armstrong (2009), there are five major career development concerns for veterans: (a) culture shock; (b) transferable skills; (c) job preparation; (d) job search concerns; and (e) financial concerns. The most difficult challenge for transitioning veterans is navigating cultural differences between the military and civilian worlds. As veterans separate from the military, many also experience the loss of their military identities. Therefore, it is important for career counselors to be sensitive to the psychological experiences of SVSM leaving the military and how these feelings may influence their career development (Simpson & Armstrong, 2009). Another common challenge for SVSM is to provide accurate explanations of their military skills and experience to potential civilian employers. Career counselors can help SVSM translate and then incorporate their military training and experience into their civilian career development. To this end, career counselors can offer classes or workshops specifically for veterans to inform them about the needs and realities of the current civilian workforce (DiRamio & Jarvis, 2011). Currently, a variety of online resources is available to translate military terminology to civilian terms (see Appendix). Career counselors can suggest these resources to SVSM so that they can learn about comparative civilian job information, including job titles, required training, hiring plans, and salary information (Simpson & Armstrong, 2009). Career counselors can support SVSM with resume and cover-letter writing, educate them about the importance of networking, and offer mock interviews. Because of their unfamiliarity with civilian jobs, many SVSM have unrealistic expectations about civilian work, including salary, job search process, and the time it takes to secure a position (Anderson, as cited in Simpson & Armstrong, 2009). Moreover, career counselors should identify the common myths about the civilian world of work held among SVSM and help them gain more realistic perspectives about civilian jobs and the job search process. Also, to enhance SVSM job search strategies, counselors should direct them to use appropriate job search tools, particularly those aimed at veterans (see Appendix).

Furthermore, many veterans experience financial anxiety associated with securing civilian employment. Career counselors should normalize the nervousness SVSM may feel while helping them to obtain appropriate information specific to certain careers (Simpson & Armstrong, 2009).

In working with SVSM, it is important for career counselors to understand the impact of their military experience on their career development (Simpson & Armstrong, 2009). For instance, when assigning service members to jobs, the military places more emphasis on specific skills and abilities than their interests and values (Clemens & Milson, 2008). Given this practice in the military, SVSM may benefit from exploring how their interests and values influence their career development (Clemens & Milson, 2008).

Career counselors should be trained to understand and recognize combat-related stress and make referrals to the counseling center when SVSM clients need treatment. SVSM are sensitive about self-disclosing their mental health difficulties due to fears of job discrimination and negative career consequences. Career counselors should respect the apprehensions of SVSM related to mental health issues and career options, and create an opportunity to discuss their concerns, possible decisions, and possible consequences of such decisions (Simpson & Armstrong, 2009).

We strongly recommend that career services create a variety of resources and opportunities for supporting SVSM career development. When developing relationships with potential business recruiters, career counselors should actively promote the benefits of employing veterans (ACE, 2013a). Developing partnerships with community organizations that serve veterans is critical for career centers to obtain important information for SVSM employment opportunities. For instance, the ACE (2013a) recommended a One-Stop Career Center and Disabled Veterans Outreach Program Specialist (DVOPS) as critical resources for providing career services to SVSM. Career centers should invite these organizations to provide career development strategy workshops. In addition, by collaborating with veterans services on campus, career services can also organize job fairs, internship fairs, round tables, and mentor programs to promote career development among SVSM.

RESIDENCE LIFE

Though SVSM may appreciate the convenience that campus residence halls typically offer all students, the age and cultural differences between typical residential students and SVSM usually creates dissonance. Furthermore, SVSM often find residence life and campus programs "irrelevant" (Francis & Kraus, 2012, p. 12). Hence, residence life staff need to consider ways that these potential learning opportunities may become more relevant. For example, allowing SVSM regardless of age or marital status to live in graduate student, married housing, or apartment style living is typically appropriate (Livingston, Scott, Havice, & Cawthon, 2012). As with other student affairs professionals, leaders of housing and residence life must ensure that their staff is informed about prevalent SVSM issues and resources that can assist when needed. This includes procedures for withdrawing from campus housing for deployed student veterans (Livingston et al., 2012). Those SVSM with PTSD who do live on campus should be warned by safety and facilities personnel of safety and emergency drills with alarms, as these may trigger flashbacks (Pellegrin, 2013). When developing and reviewing current housing policies, it is important for staff to consider that SVSM are typically older than most students and have life experiences that many will never come to understand. Therefore, a common practice in some higher education institutions is having SVSM room together. However, Livingston et al. (2012) recommended not "outing" SVSM, but allowing them to self-identify. In addition, waiving policies that require first year SVSM to live on campus should be considered given the maturity of SVSM. Staff members should understand how the SVSM housing allowance impacts decisions that SVSM may make about their living options (Uribe & Cano, 2013).

CAMPUS PROGRAMS, ORIENTATION, AND STUDENT UNION MANAGEMENT

One purpose of campus programs, orientation, and student unions is to "enhance the overall educational experience" (CAS, 2012, p. 93). Hence, understanding how SVSM experience the campus environment is important to accomplish the mission of these offices (Jackson et al., 2013). Furthermore, because SVSM is considered a diverse population, campus programs and student activities offices have the obligation to take extra steps in ensuring a supportive SVSM club or organization exists and is advised by a caring faculty or staff member with expertise. This may be particularly the case at community colleges where the typical shorter tenure of students and the increased likelihood of students being older with family and full-time job obligations makes a purely student-initiated club or organization more difficult to organize and maintain. Typical policies restricting the recognition of student groups as official organizations may need to be reviewed for traditional student age bias.

The GI Bill, though generous, has time restrictions. These "may decrease the likelihood" that SVSM will engage in student organizations and programs other than those connected with veteran status (DeSawal, 2013, p. 79). The purpose of student clubs and organizations for all students as well as SVSM is to encourage the formation of strong peer ties and meaningful relationships (DiRamio & Jarvis, 2011). Campus program staff should make substantial efforts to be sure that SVSM "find opportunities to exercise their considerable leadership skills on campus" (Francis & Kraus, 2012, p. 13). Most likely a student veteran club is advised by or at least has a relationship with the office of student or campus activities and if the student veteran club has an office space or lounge it is likely to be in the student union or center. It is the responsibility of student affairs professionals who work in these areas to provide SVSM opportunities to participate in student governance, increase leadership skills and experiences, and enhance ethical decision making (CAS, 2012). Furthermore, student affairs professionals who work in student unions must provide "an inclusive environment where interaction and understanding among individuals from diverse backgrounds occurs" (CAS, 2012, p. 178). This includes SVSM. Francis and Kraus (2012) noted that SVSM on their campus devised a credo that "nothing about us without us" (p. 15). Though in general an admirable guide, SVSM must know that "accountability for decisions always ultimately rested with professional staff" (Francis & Kraus, 2012, p. 15). Advisors of a SVSM organization should recognize that weekly meetings of SVSM provide an ongoing important support for SVSM (Schlossberg, 2011). In addition, student affairs professionals must be clear and articulate about what behaviors are acceptable in student organization office space, including the student veterans club (Francis & Kraus, 2012).

MULTICULTURAL STUDENT AFFAIRS, WOMEN'S CENTERS, AND LGBT RESOURCE CENTERS

Through experience in the military, most SVSM have significant interactions with people of a variety of cultures. SVSM have been described as "globally aware and culturally adept" (DiRamio & Jarvis, 2011, p. 40). Continuing such opportunities represents another best practice (DiRamio & Davis, 2011), especially regarding issues that pertain to social identities that are under-represented in the military (i.e., people of color, women, gay, lesbian, and transgender persons) and issues of White, male, and officer privilege (Francis & Jarvis, 2012). Therefore, self-awareness opportunities are particularly important surrounding intersecting social identities that include not only the SVSM identity (see Chapter 6) but also gender, disability, race, sexual orientation, and income (DiRamio & Jarvis, 2011). To accomplish this, collaborations between campus veterans services and multicultural student services, the women's center, and the LGBTQ resource center are imperative. These resource centers must be prepared to work with a variety of students across the political spectrum, some of who have hidden important aspects of their identities.

ASSESSMENT

Best practices in assessment include collecting data on the demographics of students served, effectiveness of programs and services, and outcomes (particularly learning) of academic endeavors (CAS, 2012). Demographics of assessments should include the identification of SVSM (DiRamio & Jarvis, 2011). Campuses must be purposeful in seeking feedback from SVSM on perceptions of campus climate and on efforts to engage with the campus community (Jackson et al., 2013). This should include surveying SVSM and veteran alumni about their experiences. Determining SVSM perceptions should occur in a variety of ways including regular and purposeful interactions with SVSM and conducting focus groups (Jackson et al., 2013). DiRamio and Jarvis (2011) complimented the *Soldier to Student* study that used factor analysis data to identify areas of focus.

Beyond the satisfaction with and effectiveness of programs and services from the perspective of SVSM, it is imperative that educators determine what it is SVSM gain from attending higher education. According to Sander (2013), Google has funded a national study to assess "veterans' academic performance and determine what kinds of campus-based programs help them most" (p. A6). Results were expected in 2014. Likewise, we recommend that veteran status be asked on institutional learning assessments. Because SVSM appear to be less likely to be engaged, they should also be identified on engagement surveys. Moreover, there appear to be inconsistent data on graduation rates of SVSM as compared to the remainder of the students. This should be clarified at each institution and also by institution type.

According to Jackson et al. (2013), important assessment questions include the following: What are best recruitment methods for this institution and what are retention rates of SVSM in comparison to other students? Are SVSM receiving specialized advising, and what are they learning from this, and what is this enabling them to do? Are there special supports for under-represented SVSM (i.e., women, LGBTQ, people of color) and how is the institution effective in retaining these students? How knowledgeable are SVSM about institutional initiatives supporting veterans? Do SVSM have access to a supportive peer network? Are supports for SVSM adequately coordinated? According to Sander (2013), recent National Survey of Student Engagement findings from 2012 indicated that SVSM find support they need to succeed academically but institutions are less likely to provide support with "nonacademic responsibilities" (p. A6) such as personal counseling.

Having opportunities to explore career aspirations of SVSM is essential. Considering the higher unemployment rates of veterans nationwide, so too is how best to connect SVSM with job opportunities. To assist in connecting SVSM with jobs, area employers should be surveyed about their needs (Francis & Kraus, 2012).

To conduct a self-assessment comparing an institution's practices against standards, institutions may wish to consult the 8th edition of the CAS Standards (2012). Institutions can also utilize the Environmental Evaluation for Veterans Index (EEVI), which offers benchmarks and is based on a "comprehensive review of published research and recommendations related to working with student veterans" (Griffith & Gilbert, 2012, p. 2). These standards and benchmarks share some similarities with ACE's veteran-friendly toolkit (2013a).

CONCLUSION

Implementing culturally appropriate best practices is the responsibility of institutions, specific educational units, and those who work in higher education. Higher education administrators, student affairs professionals, faculty, and staff must "continue the conversation on equity in higher education, we must continue to explore our boundaries and our positionality to more effectively and authentically connect not only with the student veteran population, but with all student groups" (Francis & Kraus, 2012, p. 14). This means that to more completely accomplish the mission of educating a diverse student body, those who work with SVSM must consider their own intersecting social identities and campus roles. All higher education administrators and student affairs professionals must possess "resolve to achieve the educational objectives" of all students including SVSM (DiRamio & Jarvis, 2011, p. 40–41). Best practices can provide a guide for how that can be accomplished.

In the scenario beginning this chapter, about Chris the higher education administrator and Jamie the student veteran, obviously Chris needs to initiate a process for Jamie to find an advisor. Chris may choose to address Jamie's confusion about course feedback. A competent advisor must also work to create a subsequent course schedule of a degree that Jamie sees as consistent with a life mission. An advisor should inquire about Jamie's connection to the SVSM community, campus veterans services, and other campus resources. Jamie should be reminded of the confidential counseling that is available on campus.

What learning is possible when educators enact best practices? With illustrations from our research we address this question next.

Chapter 6

Student Veteran Cognitive and Identity Development

To introduce this chapter, we open with several quotes from four SVSM participants that display a range of perspectives about their campus experiences. We begin with Henry.

> I'm like, can't I just do some push-ups and call it a day? [In the military] there is no come up with your own idea. [Instead] this is what needs to be done, do it, and then I go and do it and I do it fine . . . Veterans get frustrated, myself included, they just need someone to say "hey do this" and then they can do it . . . I'm like . . . you left me too much room, you got to give me a little more narrower street.
>
> (Henry)

> Some of the subjects had military connotations behind it; well we automatically got drawn into that material.
>
> (Bob)

> Listening to what other people have to say. [Their] ideas, you know some people have military families, some people probably don't even like the military who knows, but everybody has their own ideas. It's good to like, you know, bring them all out there, share them, put them on the table, see what comes out of it. I had actually a very interesting class, it was Arab–Israeli conflict, and there were a lot of Jewish students, there were a lot of Middle Eastern students, from different parts and there was tension, but everyone was very respectful with their own opinions. I mean it was a contentious topic but everybody was very respectful . . . I learned a lot about the background of conflict.
>
> (Miguel)

> [I had] an aha moment [when] I was in uniform and I'm coming back from training and there was a Muslim student who is very afraid of me. I could just

tell his face changed and he didn't know that I was walking the same [direction] he was going. When he saw me he was in a little bit of shock and then he turned. We see Muslim students, and then we see Muslim students. He had the hat, the dress, the beard. He was a little more orthodox than most of them [here]. I could tell he was very uncomfortable with me walking behind. It was another aha moment when I realized that a lot of them feel like we actually might be a little bit oppressive. Like we are out to get them in a way . . . So, I tried to walk slower and relax the way I was walking, be a little bit more casual about it.

(Carlos)

It may be obvious that the quotes are noteworthy because of the range of identity perspectives and complex thought they represent. We have two aims in this chapter. Because during our data collection process we heard several participants (primarily at the community college site) relay that they just needed "the piece of paper" (a degree), one aim is to expose what it is that some of our participants gained from college attendance beyond "the piece of paper." What can happen to SVSM during the process of earning their degrees? The second aim is to use student development literature to deeply understand the experiences of SVSM in college as demonstrated in the above quotes. Because it is beyond the scope of this chapter to offer a substantial background of development theory, we encourage the reader to study the sources cited here for essential knowledge of this chapter. However, we begin by reminding the reader of important concepts in student development.

CONSIDERING DEVELOPMENT HOLISTICALLY

The title of this chapter is "Student and Veteran Cognitive and Identity Development." It is crucial to recognize that though cognitive and identity development are at times considered separate concepts and processes, they are lived holistically. Harkening back to earlier theorists, Baxter Magolda (2013) lamented the failure of some theorists to recognize the "intersections of intellect, identity, and social relations" (p. xvi). An important term associated with this holistic development is meaning making. Baxter Magolda (2001) portrayed three developmental processes that are components of meaning making: cognitive (how people construct knowledge, not what they know but how they come to know it); interpersonal (how people define their relationships); and intrapersonal (how people understand themselves, including their social identities such as race, gender, sexual orientation, and social class). In their conceptual Model of Multiple Dimensions of Identity, Jones and McEwen (2000) created a figure that depicts one's central personal identity or core, surrounded by intersecting circles representing social group identities. The significance of each social identity is represented by dots being placed close to the core. Both the core and intersecting circles of group identity are located within a context. Moreover, in their Reconceptualized Model of Multiple Dimensions of Identity, Jones and Abes (2013) acknowledged that there is a "relationship between context, meaning making, and identity salience" but that the relationship is not always "neat and predictable" (p. 113). In Chapter 2 we discussed the cultural context of SVSM as they transition into and out of the military and into higher education. Here we remind the reader of the influence of cultural context in meaning making and emphasize that identities are "deeply embedded in and created out of contexts" (Jones & Abes, 2013, p. 88). In highlighting the notion that cognitive and identity development are interrelated and that development occurs holistically, in this chapter we use the concepts of cultural context, meaning making, and identity to analyze the experiences of SVSM.

Defining Identity and its Context

According to Jones and Abes (2013), identity "is produced by cultures and in interaction with the social world" and it "is always in process, unstable, and fragmented" (p. 25). In 1987, Josselson defined identity as an "unconscious process that unites the personality and links the individual with the social world . . . preserving the continuity of the self, linking the past with the present . . . Identity becomes a way for people to organize and understand their experience and share that with others" (pp. 10–11). This definition also offers a holistic view of development; involving interpersonal, intrapersonal, and cognitive processes.

It is clear that context influences identity. Contextual influences include "family background, sociocultural conditions, current life experiences, and career decisions and life planning" (Jones & McEwen, 2000, p. 410). These can constrain self-perceptions. Jones and McEwen wrote:

> When identities are imposed from the outside, dimensions are not seen as integral to the core. However, when interacting with certain sociocultural conditions such as sexism and racism, identity dimensions may be scrutinized in a new way that resulted in participants' reflection and greater understanding of a particular dimension.
>
> (p. 410)

In considering environment as context, Torres, Jones, and Renn (2009) wrote, "The role of environment in identity development remains undertheorized and understudied" (p. 591). Later in this chapter, we offer an example of how the higher education context influences development.

Jones and Abes (2013) acknowledged that there are both personal and social aspects of identity: personal in that there is an individual distinctive draw to a group or groups, and social in that a person asserts membership with others in a group or groups. Similarly, Josselson's (1987) definition above includes both personal and social claims to identity.

Social Identity

Many definitions of social identities emphasize the human construction of groups (e.g., gender, race, ethnicity, sexual orientation, socioeconomic class). Additionally, Jones and Abes (2013) wrote that "social identities are influenced by social constructions that emerge from structures of privilege and oppression" (p. 40). In other words, when people feel alone or isolated, they will seek out support from others who also experience similar contextual isolation. Social identities that are less privileged in the environment tend to become more salient.

Several researchers have studied the notion of veteran or student veteran as a social identity. Harada et al. (2002) defined the identity dimension of veteran as the self-concept that derives from military experience within a context of the social and historical tradition of the military. Barón (2014) differentiated the social identity of student veteran from the label. The label of student veteran is one of convenience and is a descriptive characteristic, but lacks specificity, whereas the social identity of student veteran is a means to connect with like others. However, student veterans' experiences are so varied that the term student veteran has little individual meaning for some. Zinger and Cohen (2010) emphasized that for some student veterans the identity task is integrating the two selves (student and veteran) to become one whole person.

In writing about women SVSM, Baechtold and DeSawal (2009) claimed that an identity crisis occurs when the "military occupation is removed and a new vocation must be found" (p. 40). Women must construct "a new identity that is specifically related to gender in order to make meaning of the college environment" (p. 40).

Contrarily, some veterans lament the notion of being treated as a special or identity group (Hassan, Jackson, Lindsay, McCabe, & Sanders, 2010). Hassan et al. (2010) prefer to emphasize the strengths and assets veterans bring to higher education rather than perceived and real needs. Members of other groups also lament deficit models that are often used to describe them. The point is to create environments that empower students to achieve more than they thought possible (Hassan et al., 2010).

External and Internal Influence

Whether or when a person uses external and internal influences in making sense of their world is an essential concept in student development (and of course an individualistic culture) (Baxter Magolda, 2001). For example, is the source of knowledge strictly from external authorities or are multiple standpoints taken into consideration, including an internal one (Jones & Abes, 2013)? In relationships, when does one party control the other or are the roles, rights, and responsibilities in relationships consistently respectful and mutually beneficial

(Kegan, 1994)? Is a person defined by relationships, or if a relationship ended would there still be a functioning self (Kegan, 1994)? Is one's identity often based on external sources of notions of who one should be, or does the sense of self include internally driven perspectives (Baxter Magolda, 2001)? Are the cognitive, interpersonal, and intrapersonal components of development described above in polar oppositions of external versus internal influences? Or is there a dynamic interplay between external and internal influences (Jones & Abes, 2013)? The degree of external and internal contexts influence the meaning-making capacity which filters how and what social identities are deemed central to the core sense of self (Abes, Jones, & McEwen, 2007) (see Figure 6.1). This is described in greater degree below. It is with these concepts of student development in mind that we return to our participants' perspectives.

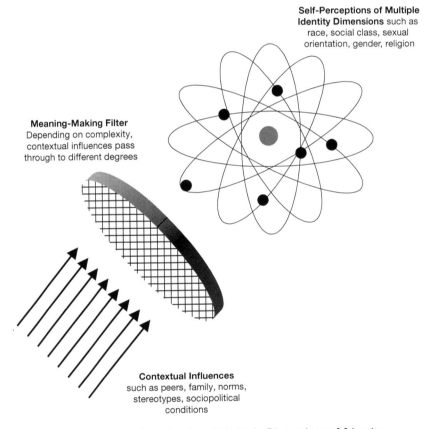

Self-Perceptions of Multiple Identity Dimensions such as race, social class, sexual orientation, gender, religion

Meaning-Making Filter Depending on complexity, contextual influences pass through to different degrees

Contextual Influences such as peers, family, norms, stereotypes, sociopolitical conditions

Figure 6.1 Reconceptualized Model of Multiple Dimensions of Identity

Source: From Abes, Jones, and McEwen, 2007, American College Personnel Association, reprinted with permission

MOVING INTO HIGHER EDUCATION: "BABY FACES"

In our research, we found that SVSM often have taken college courses either before entering the military or during their military experience. In fact, very few SVSM had not taken a college course before arriving at their current institution. Therefore these SVSM do not view themselves as new students. Moreover, our research confirmed the research of others (DiRamio & Jarvis, 2011; Rumann & Hamrick, 2010) that SVSM see themselves as more mature and competent than other students. One SVSM at a community college stated that students "are broken into two sections. You've either got your adult learners or you've got your baby faces, fresh out of high school." Another stated:

> I think it is good in a sense that I missed out on the phase that a lot of my peers are in now where they are 18 and they just, well a lot of them seem pretty well off. So they just left home and they are just out of mom and dad's reach so a lot of them are doing stupid things like missing class, coming in late every day, or coming in without their books.

Though acknowledging classmates as "my peers" in the above quote, the dichotomous comparisons of veterans with their student peers were common at CC and RI. Moreover, several veterans in our study used the term "normal" to describe younger traditional students. For example, Alan stated, "with normal students it's like deployment, they wouldn't really understand." In contrast to the "baby faces," veterans described themselves as experienced, committed, and mature. According to Miguel, "we know what we want, we just need the credentials to match our goals." Steven indicated that:

> veterans stand out [because] they are a little more disciplined . . . [There is] a different perspective as far as pride in the environment . . . Hey, you know, clean that stuff up you know there is a cigarette butt container there . . . that's a big thing in the military, policing after yourself.

These remarks demonstrate several points. First, some veterans view themselves and their peers as opposites on a polarized continuum. This dualistic view is described by Perry (1981) as a form of dichotomous thinking and within that dichotomy some veterans see other students as "normal," implying that they are abnormal. But, through this abnormalcy, they have become competent. Chickering and Reisser (1993) described three aspects of competence – intellectual, physical and manual skills, and interpersonal – all of which are encompassed in the seven vectors of identity. Chickering and Reisser wrote that competence "stems from the confidence that one can cope with what comes and achieve goals successfully" (p. 53). In our findings we saw evidence of this

COGNITIVE AND IDENTITY DEVELOPMENT

confidence and competence, particularly intellectual and physical. We also saw evidence that SVSM achieved interpersonal competence in the military context but less so in the higher education context. The salience of context to identity is obvious here (Jones & Abes, 2013). The military is still the context that influences the filter for how SVSM view themselves and others. The judgments of these SVSM are based on a dualistic view of how civilian student classmates might complete boot camp, not a course or degree in higher education. In discussing "baby faces," we heard little evidence of significant interaction with faculty, staff, or students except with other SVSM. This perspective is an interpersonal, intrapersonal, and cognitive example of Berry's (2005) separation/segregation strategy referred to in Chapter 2. This is highlighted in Bob's statement above that "[s]ome of the subjects had military connotations behind it; well we automatically got drawn into that material." Participants were "automatically drawn" into material that was familiar and comfortable. Certainly this is similar to other students who feel new and isolated; they take comfort in the familiar.

We could have easily titled this section "Can't I just do some push-ups and call it a day?" Although participants often referred to their classmates as "baby faces" they also lamented not being told what to do. The experience of faculty and staff members leaving "too much room" and Henry wanting "a little more narrower street" illustrate the comfort with external influences for generating knowledge and the discomfort in using the internal self to construct knowledge from multiple sources. Certainly Henry and Bob are competent students. Among other tasks, they are capable of manipulating complex equipment, following complex instructions, and surviving away from family and home culture. Baxter Magolda (2011) urged higher education to ask more of students and to implement learning opportunities (such as active learning pedagogies) that prompt internal sources of meaning making or what Baxter Magolda (2001) and Kegan (1994) called self-authorship. According to Kegan, "a *self-authorship* can coordinate, integrate, act upon, or invent values, beliefs, convictions, generalizations, ideals, abstractions, interpersonal loyalties, and intrapersonal states" (1994, p. 185). Whether because of development or because of transitioning to their new environment, Henry and Bob's statements indicate a struggle to "construct one's own point of view" (Kegan, 1994, p. 39).

In his poignant book *In Over Our Heads: The Mental Demands of Modern Life*, Kegan (1994) described the complex cognitive capacities required to live a contented and informed life. He proposed five knowledge structures or orders of consciousness of increasing complexity. The orders are framed around "important features" (Kegan, 1994, p. 32). These features include the organization of how one constructs experiences "including one's thinking, feeling, and social-relating" (p. 32). Baxter Magolda (2001) believed that most college students use Kegan's third order of consciousness. In this knowledge structure, students do not yet have ideas about their ideas (Kegan, 1994). They construct values and ideas, but they subordinate their own interest on behalf of loyalty to others. In fact, meaningful others' opinions matter to a fundamental extent. Thinking from the third order of consciousness is directed by students' personal history. In working with others, they tend to own the work of others. They are as worried about the work of others as they are their own work. They do not have a relationship with others' work; they are others' work. Consider the conflicts that often surround student group projects in which students whose knowledge structures are not yet at the third order of consciousness care too little about the group project but others care too much about the work of others in the group.

We believe Henry and Bob's comments reflect third order consciousness thinking. Bob is drawn into material that is familiar and comfortable when so much around him is unfamiliar. However, Kegan might ask whether there is any "psychological independence" (p. 111) here, or in other words internal meaning making. Henry and Bob are experiencing higher education through their previous military structure, one where independence is not valued or expected. It is through this structure that they make meaning of their identity.

A significant determining factor of whether or not SVSM connect and integrate with the campus community was if they had experienced what participants often referred to as "bad stuff" or "raw subjects." "Bad stuff" and "raw subjects" was a contextual factor that influenced the meaning-making filter. It also determined if there were external, internal, or evolving influences on meaning making.

LEARNING THROUGH "BAD STUFF" AND "RAW SUBJECTS"

Here we describe an important unique contextual factor that our SVSM participants brought with them to campus. We use phrases uttered by participants: "bad stuff" and "raw subjects." Even before we interviewed her, one participant indicated that she was afraid she would not be an informative participant because she had not experienced the "bad stuff." We asked what she meant. To her it meant not experiencing the horrors that come with combat. Lair (2011) described consumerism and soldiering in Vietnam and provided data indicating that increasingly fewer military personnel are assigned to combat zones. In Iraq and Afghanistan, more military personnel than ever serve in support roles. Though conditions in combat zones can be ghastly and take a serious toll on personnel involved in combat (as described in Chapter 7), according to Lair they are a decreasing percentage of the war experience and make "it easier to go to war again and again and again" (p. 247). Nonetheless, some of the participants in our study did experience "bad stuff." Though we did not initiate the topic, participants discussed this mostly in implicit ways. Bob stated that "I know our government does stuff that people shouldn't know about. The wolves have to be out there to guard the sheep for a reason." Another participant, Steven, a nursing student, mused, "I have seen enough blood and guts; that stuff doesn't bother me." Henry described his experiences of doing things

you can't do when you are around a normal society and I have spent a lot of time in the woods and in the desert living like a pig basically because you're living out in the middle of nowhere, which you kind of get back into the fact that you are a civilized people. You don't live in a hole in the ground. You have to clean up.

When describing the right of passage to earn a degree, Steven inserted the "bad stuff" this way, "A piece of paper . . . was given because people were willing to, you know, go someplace else and do bad things so that we can continue to have the environment that we have here." Jerry poignantly described the "bad stuff" this way, "I felt like a monster . . . Frankenstein or something . . . like the level of violence that I have experienced and what I have seen was nothing they [student non-veteran peers] could even imagine." As might be expected, some SVSM recalled their experiences of being asked by peer college students if they had ever shot or killed anyone. In addressing his "bad stuff," Carlos related that:

One time I was out having beers with friends from one of my classes and a girl said, "So you shot people, you were shooting people. I can't believe I'm sitting here with somebody who actually shot people." She didn't say it in a bad way. She, I guess, had her own aha moment, right. Like, "Oh my God" this is what we do . . . To me it was like "Oh my gosh" this is what people really think about me.

But for Jerry, the "bad stuff" took its toll.

I was not really participating in classes, sitting there in the back, I just felt isolated and wounded . . . that was the period of time I found out that I was diagnosed with PTSD. I started focusing on myself, getting better . . . just hanging out in the gym, exercising, met some people at the gym, cut out drinking.

Besides the concept of "bad stuff," we found evidence of "raw subjects." We heard more of this phenomenon at CC than at RI. This term was first used by a SVSM who had a conflict with a faculty member who remarked in class that the government's response to 9/11 "caused more disaster" than the attacks themselves. The participant told us that the faculty member

[c]ould tell that he agitated us, so the three of us stayed after to talk to him and he was like, "I'm not doing this as a poke towards the military. I fully

support the military and I'll never talk bad about them, but the government is not the military." We got to the understanding; it's just a raw subject for any vet.

(Bob)

The coordinator of veterans affairs at the CC institution said that faculty sometimes intimidate younger SVSM and that some faculty "call veterans out." Participants there lamented faculty who seemed biased against SVSM and who saw SVSM as being government agents. SVSM responded to experiences such as this by maintaining their military identity. Arthur, a vice president of student affairs at one of the campuses of RI, indicated that veterans there wanted "to control how their story is told." These are the contexts within which some SVSM transition into higher education.

SVSM come from environments where they are immersed with other military members then enter into higher education institutions where they are a small percentage of the student population. We found in our study that those participants who had experienced the "bad stuff," "raw subjects," and were repeatedly asked about killing people were more likely to view their military identity as close to their core in the higher education environment. This confirms Jones and McEwen's (2000) findings that aspects of the self closest to the core are often what are experienced as a different or outsider identity in the environment. DiRamio and Jarvis (2011) used the term "skeptic" to describe the phenomenon where SVSM "live with a continuing commitment to a military core identity, which serves as their dominant sense of self" (p. 62). Lang (2013) described his isolation this way:

As I walked to the college it was nothing like what I had expected. The stares I received (or felt) from other students gave me an empty feeling in my stomach. I counted the minutes until class was over and sat close to the door so I could leave soon as class was dismissed.

(p. 40)

In the Reconceptualized Model of Multiple Dimensions of Identity, Abes et al. (2007) added a meaning-making filter to their previous model through which students strain their experiences and identity. The meaning-making filter influences how students see their core. A filter may allow much of the outside world such as "peers, family, norms, stereotypes, sociopolitical conditions" (Abes et al., 2007, p. 7) to influence their self-perception. Abes et al. (2007) presented evidence that a filter could allow more or less external influences of the self. Narrowing the filter lessens the susceptibility to external influences and instead allows a more personal view of the self. Abes et al. (2007) noted that students begin to "realize the limitations of stereotypes [and] feel frustrated by identity

101

labels" (p. 9). Baxter Magolda (2001) and Kegan (1994) believe this occurs in a transitional way. Some participants in our study who found supportive faculty, student affairs professionals, higher education administrators, and staff also described their military identity as close to their core, but this seemed to be a temporary condition, occurring while they adjusted to the academic culture and environment. Abes et al. (2007) also found that students "were adept at resisting stereotypes and typically presented their identity in a consistent manner regardless of the environment" (2007, p. 11). Holding the veteran identity close to their core confirms findings of other research about SVSM. What we suggest here is, being asked frequently about killing maintained the military context in influencing the SVSM identity and was a deterrent to being integrated into the college community. In Rumann and Hamrick's (2010) research, another stereotype, the hero, required "filtering out . . . their own evolving senses of self" (p. 453). Both these killer and hero characterizations highlight SVSM differences from other students and influence the internal view of self and with whom they have relationships. The combat context influences the meaning-making filter through which SVSM understand their place in the world. With reflection on their experiences, SVSM can and do begin to use other contexts to influence their filter and their view of the self.

RESPONDING TO "AN AHA MOMENT"

A critical component of Kegan's (1994) research is the subject–object relationship. Here, object means those "elements of our knowing or organizing that we can reflect on, handle, look at, be responsible for, relate to each other, take control of, internalize, assimilate, or otherwise operate upon" (p. 32), whereas subject "refers to those elements of our knowing or organizing that we are identified with, tied to, fused with, or embedded in" (p. 32). Kegan added, "we *have* object; we *are* subject" (p. 32, emphasis in original). As people grow in the complexity of their mental organization, "that which was subject becomes object" (p. 33). Do we "have it" or are we "had by it" (p. 34)? He offered asking people across age ranges to describe what the movie *Star Wars* is about as demonstrating the range of complex cognitive organization structures. Is the response a chronological depiction of what happened or an "abstraction" about the "battle between good and evil" (p. 33)? Such answers demonstrate one's cognitive structure.

We return to Miguel's statements that began this chapter.

Listening to what other people have to say. Their ideas, you know some people have military families, some people probably don't even like the military, who knows, but everybody has their own ideas. It's good to like, you know, bring them all out there, share them, put them on the table, see what comes out of it. I had actually a very interesting class, it was Arab–Israeli conflict, and there were a lot of Jewish students, there were a lot of Middle Eastern students, from different parts and there was tension, but everyone was very respectful with their own opinions. I mean it was a contentious topic but everybody was very respectful . . . I learned a lot about the background of conflict.

Miguel's quote about his course in conflict analysis demonstrates his ability to reflect on the discourse of others (object) rather than be the discourse (subject). He is comfortable listening to others, even if they do not like him. How they feel about his being a veteran or veterans in general is not essential to him. He is more intrigued by the demonstration of respect by others' poignant "ideas" that are "out on the table." According to Miguel, all students in the class can have a relationship to the "ideas" rather than being had by them. Kegan might tell us that Miguel was beginning to experience higher education through a fourth order of consciousness. In the fourth order of consciousness, people begin to break with what they thought were infallible external guides and position this guidance outside of themselves. In the fourth order of consciousness people begin not to hold others responsible for their experiences of unhappiness. They come to be productive about personal histories and have values about their values. People who make meaning through the fourth order of consciousness place limits on relationships and those they love without feeling guilty about it. Likewise, they do not stop caring for others but do stop being made up by their caring. Through this structure people *have* duties (object) rather than *are* those duties (subject). These people have more direct communication. In work and leadership roles these people are responsible for their own roles and supervise others' roles, but they also monitor their own responses to those roles. They evaluate their own performance and initiate changes to their performance based on their own critique (object). They understand that some important aspects of their lives are beyond their control. From the fourth order of consciousness people are self-authored (Kegan, 1994).

In Miguel's quote we can hear that he is able to step outside his own opinions and view his along with those of his classmates. His filter for viewing the world and himself within it is more open to a wide range of views. Though he does not indicate he has changed his ideas because of others' ideas, he is able to recognize that his are not universal; nor should they be. Instead of being offended by others' ideas he is intrigued by them and even has learned from them. He now believes it is good to share them, bring them out, shake them around, and just see what happens. His world is less structured and he is fine with it. The external and internal influences engage here. Miguel is shaking up these ideas in his mind. But, he does not indicate any conclusions he has reached. He even seems surprised by his interest. Furthermore, he is not doing anything differently because of his new learning. He is an audience member watching his Muslim and Israeli classmates debate, rather than an active participant. In contrast, writing about Bloom's hierarchy of learning, Armstrong (2014) emphasized learning as an active endeavor. This brings us to discuss Carlos. Carlos related a poignant incident. He told us:

> [I had] an aha moment [when] I was in uniform and I'm coming back from training and there was a Muslim student who is very afraid of me. I could just tell his face changed and he didn't know that I was walking the same [direction] he was going. When he saw me he was in a little bit of shock and then he turned. We see Muslim students, and then we see Muslim students. He had the hat, the dress, the beard. He was a little more orthodox than most of them [here]. I could tell he was very uncomfortable with me walking behind. It was another aha moment when I realized that a lot of them feel like we actually might be a little bit oppressive. Like we are out to get them in a way . . . So, I tried to walk slower and relax the way I was walking, be a little bit more casual about it.

There is much richness in Carlos's story. Baxter Magolda (2013) cited Kegan's 1982 book *The Evolving Self: Problem and Process on Human Development* that "people make meaning '*between* an event and a reaction to it—the place where the event is privately composed, made sense of, the place where it actually becomes an event for a person'" (Baxter Magolda, 2013, p. xv) (emphasis in original). Certainly, Carlos makes a great deal of meaning in the reaction he perceives the Muslim student makes of him hurrying in his uniform. In this one episode of self-awareness, we see examples of fourth order consciousness and glimmers of what Kegan (1994) called his fifth order of consciousness. From the fourth order Carlos demonstrates that he has broken with an infallible external guide, he evaluated his own action, and acted upon his values. From the fifth order of consciousness Carlos was able to try on others' perspectives and discovered something about himself. Carlos begins to see himself and others beyond a single system.

Kegan (1994) maintained that contemporary society does not encourage people to use a fifth order of consciousness knowledge structure. Other aspects of this fifth order knowledge structure that Kegan would hope more adults attain include that in conflict they refuse to see only two sides and refuse to be put into a position where they are expected to take the opposite position. Adults using this complex knowledge structure consider a variety of ways of doing something. In concluding his treatise, Kegan ended with,

> Those who long for more fifth order consciousness – for the recognition of our multiple selves, for the capacity to see conflict as a signal of our over-

identification with a single system, for the sense of our relationships and connections as prior to and constitutive of the individual self, for an identification with the transformative process of our being rather than the formative products of our becoming – let them take heart . . . Are we living longer as a species precisely so that we might evolve to the fifth order?

(pp. 351–352)

Jones and Abes (2013) described a prism of privilege and difference. The prism "illuminates the influence of contextual factors that both shape and press, or push and pull on, multiple dimensions of identity, and contribute to an understanding of identity development as a dynamic, evolving process continually shaped by these many contexts" (Jones & Abes, p. 86). Through the prism of privilege Carlos is able to reflect on and speak to what his uniform and his identity may mean to others. Though he lessens the language to "a little bit oppressive," Carlos is aware of the impact of his behavior and decides to alter it. His insight makes this an event. Beyond not being consumed by this encounter, Carlos is not angered by the Muslim student's reaction, nor does he feel he has to become this student's opposite. Rather, he chooses another option. He chooses to alter his behavior in hopes that the new behavior will make another member of the community feel safer. By his slowing down, he takes responsibility for being a community member. He becomes less of the uniform he is wearing; it is a uniform (object), it is not all that he is (subject), though it remains an important aspect of who he is. His own internal meaning making of deciding to walk more slowly represents to us that his identity as college student community member has become closer to his salient identity core.

It may not be coincidental that Miguel and Carlos are men of color and Henry and Bob are two White men. Perhaps Miguel and Carlos's own experiences with racial oppression may have influenced their meaning-making filters and hence their multiple identities (veteran men of color). Also, it may be through the prism of privilege and oppression that SVSM, particularly those who are heterosexual White men, view their higher education experience in opposition to their previous military experiences. Perhaps many of these men have had few experiences of feeling isolated and powerless before coming to campus. So, how does this development analysis contribute to higher education practice?

ENCOURAGING SVSM DEVELOPMENT

In this chapter we used the contributions of development theory to more deeply understand the isolation SVSM often feel as outsiders in higher education. Similar to DiRamio and Jarvis (2011), we used a developmental viewpoint on our participants' experiences. We brought clarity into how knowledge structures, stereotypes, SVSM perceptions of biased faculty, and the prism of privilege and oppression can influence SVSM development. Miguel and Carlos also illustrate the potential of a higher education experience. We provided evidence of the type of learning that can occur that is beyond a piece of paper. We demonstrated the connectedness to course ideas and college community members that can occur over time. Indeed, veteran identity is salient to the core sense of self of SVSM particularly in the beginning of their transition, but meaning-making structures can evolve that influence the core sense of self.

What might these differing SVSM perspectives suggest to higher education administrators, student affairs professionals, faculty, and staff? These perspectives imply that a supportive environment matters to SVSM, which includes opportunities to interact with like others. These perspectives also demonstrate how diversity of students, faculty, staff, and ideas influence and prompt learning. There is significant literature extolling the learning gains of honest dialogue between diverse students (Chang, 2002; Milem et al., 2005). Opportunities for such dialogues must be increased. Collaborations between campus veterans services and diverse group resource centers (as discussed in previous chapters) must be promulgated. So too must opportunities for transformative learning.

In their work on transformative learning of adults, Kroth and Boverie (2000) found that transformative learning begins with a "disorienting dilemma" (p. 144). We believe higher education offers important disorienting dilemmas as demonstrated by the quotes of SVSM in this chapter. Kroth and Boverie's writing on working and core life missions (mentioned in Chapter 5 under best practices for advising) is an example of Baxter Magolda's (2001) education partnership. Regardless of the disorienting dilemmas, Kroth and Boverie found that an adult's core life mission remains relatively unchanged throughout life. The core life mission is a theme that is central to the person. It addresses the question of "Why am I?" (Kroth & Boverie, 2000, p. 145). However, an adult may be unaware of this core mission and only become aware through significant development processes, such as those we have discussed in this chapter. Persons who work with SVSM should address both working and core life missions. Some SVSM whose meaning-making filter is open to mostly external authorities may only be concerned with the working mission. Educators should empower SVSM to take the lead in determining a working mission that is consistent with their core life mission (Kroth & Boverie, 2000; Wilson & Smith, 2012).

Lastly, this chapter offers cautions to educators about assumptions. As with other diverse student groups, educators should not assume how closely SVSM will identify with the student or veteran aspect of student veteran identity (Barón, 2014). Obviously the military experience influences the college experience, but how it does depends on the individual and his or her experiences and contexts. For example, Ann's experiences were very individual. She found the Army National Guard to be less structured than higher education. Moreover she said:

[W]hen I went over there [Iraq] it was a whole different light. I went over there and I was challenged in different ways . . . One of my sergeants came up to talk to me. This was the most challenging phrase I ever heard in my life. He said, "You have so much potential." And that changed everything.

From that one comment she took on leadership roles and decided to run a marathon. Obviously a trust ensued. The first people she ever came out to as a lesbian were her military colleagues. She found that she became close to them quickly and became comfortable with them. Subsequently, she told "these two guys and they told everybody . . . but honestly nobody really talked about it . . . nobody cared."

Previously we highlighted cultural differences between the military and higher education cultures. Though Ann's experiences as an out lesbian woman of color were exceedingly positive in the military, other SVSM describe the emphasis on equity issues in higher education to be one of the cultural differences they experience. We focus in the next chapter on how equity issues experienced in the military influence higher education.

Chapter 7

Equity Issues

Pat is 21, a student in a public university, but like thousands of other young people decides to leave college to join the military. What motivates Pat to leave college and join a complex, bureaucratic, yet proud organization with rich traditions, some older than the United States itself? What is likely to be Pat's experience in the military? How do Pat's intersecting identities influence the military experience? And most importantly for this book, how do these experiences influence Pat's return to higher education after leaving the military? This chapter addresses these questions that center on identity and equity in a hyper-masculine organization and the subsequent implications for higher education. We describe the diversity within the military and veteran populations. Then, we examine how social identities (i.e. class, race, gender, sexual orientation) influence the motivation for joining the military and experiences in the military, and ponder how social identities affect the transition to the civilian world. Lastly, we suggest implications for higher education.

At the outset, it is important to declare that social status in the military is first and foremost established by rank. Most persons in the United States are acquainted with the rigid hierarchy of rank in the military (Christian et al., 2009). Within every work group or unit who is senior, either by rank or by seniority, is quickly recognized. This has several implications. First, everyone in the military (if they serve long enough) will gain some leadership experience as well as learn how to follow. It also means that those at the lower ranks have very little power. Christian et al. (2009) acknowledged the assumption of rigid roles and unquestioning loyalty to those of higher rank, particularly officers. This unquestioning loyalty influences working and social relationships and is believed to engender trust. Yet, in organizations where some members have significantly more power than others, particularly if that power is based not only on rank but also on social identity, there can be clashes with notions of equity.

WHO JOINS THE MILITARY?

When the U.S. created an all-voluntary military in 1973 (Segal, Thanner, & Segal, 2007), a number of researchers became interested in the demographics of who served and why (MacLean & Parsons, 2010; Segal et al., 2007). Hence, there are available data on how the demographics of service members and their experiences have changed over the decades (Antecol & Cobb-Clark, 2009; Kennedy & Malone, 2009; Lundquist, 2008; Segal et al., 2007). To understand the diversity within the SVSM population, we briefly describe the recent military and veteran populations from the perspectives of gender, race, and sexual orientation.

It was immediately apparent that scholars and military planners did not expect to see an increase in women joining the military but rather expected "the burden of fighting America's wars" to be placed on the urban poor (Segal et al., 2007, p. 49). According to the U.S. Department of Veterans Affairs (2013e), there were over 2,000,500 women veterans in 2011, representing 9.8% of the total U.S. veteran population. Of those women veterans 34.1% were women of color, in comparison to 19.1% of the men. Women are a fast-growing group in the veteran population, and the number of women veterans is expected to grow to 15% by 2035 (U.S. Department of Veterans Affairs, 2011). In 2012, women comprised 14.6% of active duty forces and 18.2% of the National Guard and Reserve forces (U.S. Department of Defense, 2012). The number of women deployed in a time of war increased from 41,000 in the Gulf War to over 200,000 during Operation Enduring Freedom (OEF), Operation Iraqi Freedom (OIF), and Operation New Dawn (U.S. Department of Veterans Affairs, 2011).

In 2014, 66% of the total veteran population were White people, 16% Black, 10% Hispanic, 4% Asian, and 4% "other" (U.S. Department of Veterans Affairs, 2014b). Note that figures for American Indians are not given. In 2012, 30.3% of active duty personnel and 24.5% of Reserves and Guards were people of color and the number continues to increase among the ranks of both enlisted and officers (U.S. Department of Defense, 2012). Black service members comprise the largest active duty group of color, 16.8% (U.S. Department of Defense, 2012; U.S. Department of Veterans Affairs, 2014b).

Due to a long history of the military's exclusion policy towards lesbian, gay, bisexual, and transgender (LGBT) people, there are no official data available for this population in the military. Yet, according to Gates (2004), there are nearly one million gay and lesbian veterans in the United States. In 2010, Gates estimated that approximately 71,000 lesbian, gay, and bisexual (LGB) men and women were serving in the military. The LGB population comprises 2.2% of all military personnel, with 13,000 (0.9%) active duty personnel and 58,000 (3.4%) of National Guard and Reserves. Lesbian and bisexual women are a substantially higher portion of the military (6.2%) than gay and bisexual men (1.5%) (Gates, 2010).

Research indicates higher rates of military service among transgender people than the cisgender (non-transgender) population. In a study by Shipherd, Mizock, Maguen, and Green (2012), 30% of the male-to-female transgender participants were veterans, a rate triple that of the general population (10.1%). Based on clinical work with transgender service members, Brown (1988) and McDuffie and Brown (2010) reported high rates of military service among male-to-female transgender clients. Bryant and Schilt (2008) surveyed 827 transgender service members and veterans and found that 52% of the sample identified as female, 28% as male, 10% as other, 4% as undefined, 3% as intersex, and 3% as neutral; 38% served in the Army and 29% in the Navy. Participants represented a full range of ranks, and 47% had served in a combat zone; 86% were honorably discharged (Bryant & Schilt, 2008).

WHY JOIN?: DIFFERENCES BY DEMOGRAPHICS

Certainly economic factors in the civilian workforce influence who joins and why. For example, Lundquist (2008) noted that women of color tend to outnumber their male counterparts in the military, because "they are doubly-disadvantaged in the civilian labor market by race and gender" (p. 55). Women of color and White women join because they believe there are more opportunities for leadership in the military than in the civilian workplace (Lundquist, 2008). Also, some researchers argue that a number of women who enlist may be escaping an abusive and violent home environment because of the high prevalence of childhood sexual trauma by parental figures among women veterans and service members compared to civilian women (Schults, Bell, Naugle, & Polusrry, 2006). This is despite the acknowledgement of rampant sexual harassment of women in the military (Pryce, Pryce, & Shackelford, 2012). Perceptions of better opportunities in the military are based on the racially integrated work and living environments within the military, enforcement of equal opportunity policies, hierarchy that is based on military rank rather than race, and a disproportionate number of persons of color working and living in the military environment (Lundquist, 2008; Segal et al., 2007). The social advantages of integrated on-base housing with resources and support services have an attractive appeal, particularly to service members of color (Lundquist, 2008). In fact, Lundquist noted that on-base living may offer a "respite from racially segregated civilian military life" (p. 492) and that "structural inequality in civilian life makes a bigger difference in military job satisfaction" than race or gender (p. 493). It behooves higher education administrators and student affairs professionals to consider how this might influence SVSM of color as they return to higher education in the civilian world.

Segal et al. (2007) believed that joining the military for people of color is less influenced by culture than it is by "labor market dynamics" (p. 57). In other words, the perception of whether one can obtain a good job is statistically a more predictive factor in joining the military than whether one's father joined or one's racial group. However, demographics do play a role. As the Latino populations increase in the U.S. so too does the number of Latinos serving in the military (Segal et al., 2007). Hence, the U.S. Army has targeted Latino/a youth, spending time in communities with potential recruits' families, in particular their mothers (Segal et al., 2007). Contrarily, White recruits are more likely to list "to serve my country" as a reason for joining than economic reasons (Segal et al., 2007, p. 60). Although Latino/as in the military are less likely to have a father serving in the military than Black and White military personnel, they are more likely to have a wife who serves (Segal et al., 2007).

Within the LGBT population, the culture of hyper-masculinity in the military seems to have a significant impact on attracting transgender people. The term "flight into hyper-masculinity" was developed by Brown (1988) to describe a developmental journey common among male-to-female transgender people in an attempt to hide any transgender feelings and thoughts by submerging themselves in the hyper-masculine environment of the military, which is intolerant of any obscuring of gender boundaries (McDuffie & Brown, 2010). The culture of hyper-masculinity in the military may also be attractive for female-to-male transgender people because it is an acceptable, thus a safer, place for them to experiment with male gender behaviors (Yerke & Mitchell, 2013). In response to gender confusion during transgender identity development, these choices may be conscious or subconscious (McDuffie & Brown, 2010).

Once people join the military, what are the experiences of those who serve? How do these experiences influence their experience in higher education? Below we examine the influence of class, race, gender, and sexual orientation on service members' experiences in the military.

EXPERIENCES IN THE MILITARY

The experiences people have in the military are as varied as the people themselves. In this section we briefly discuss those experiences related to equity that we believe are most important to higher education administrators and student affairs professionals. We begin with the most dangerous aspect of military life: combat and its relationship with social class. We then turn to the effects of the masculine culture, discrimination in the military, social identity in transition, and the physical and psychological effects of serving.

Combat and Socioeconomic Class

Historically, working-class people were more likely to fight and die in American wars (Lair, 2011). Part of this was due to being "less able or willing to exploit loopholes in the draft system" (p. 18). People from families with more resources are more likely to use social power to navigate bureaucracies both in and out of the military to allow them to avoid combat. Indeed, Lair (2011) noted that knowing how to type during Vietnam could be a lifesaver.

Those in the military who are more educated tend to be more satisfied (Lundquist, 2008) and are less likely to serve in combat roles (MacLean & Parsons, 2010). Those who do serve in combat roles are more likely to be Latino, have poorer high school grades, and come from less prosperous families (MacLean & Parsons, 2010; Segal et al., 2007). In today's military, one's rate (job) is often determined by test scores. In the Vietnam era, the college educated and those from the middle and wealthy classes were underrepresented in the military. However, young Americans continue to believe that military service is an avenue to move to a higher social-economic class. According to Lair, this understanding was "cultivated by military authorities" (p. 19). We believe this still continues today and that institutions of higher education play an important role in this cultivation. By eagerly accepting SVSM as students and their GI benefits, institutions contribute their own spin on both military service and higher education as avenues to social mobility. However, there are disparities between the equity of result and the equity of opportunity (MacLean & Parsons, 2010), meaning that those who seek education through the enticing educational benefits of military service continue to face difficult hurdles in making social mobility a reality. In essence, those with needed or specialized civilian skills are less likely to serve in combat roles. Because combat roles have less transferability to civilian jobs, veterans who served in combat are more likely to be under- and unemployed as veterans (MacLean & Parsons, 2010) and their families are less likely to have resources to support them. Hence, the reward of social mobility, though attainable, becomes less likely.

Lair (2011) reported that during the Vietnam War sons of important politically connected men were on watch lists. Commanders were to refrain from having these listed sons serve in dangerous positions. Such discriminatory watch lists brewed resentment and low morale in less politically precious sons. In today's Army, there is still the intersection of race, ethnicity, class, and high school achievement. For example, Latinos are overrepresented in combat by 85% (Segal et al., 2007). This raises the question of the role that the dream of social mobility and the hope of escaping discrimination play in SVSM who enroll in higher education.

Navigating the Masculine Culture in the Military

One of the fundamental issues that affects the experience of women as well as LGBT service members in the military is the need to navigate the masculine culture. As described in Chapter 2, the military promotes traditional masculine behaviors such as emotional control (Green et al., 2010), overt heterosexual desire, physical fitness, willingness to use aggression and physical violence, and risk taking (Barrett, 1996: Brooks, 2001: Higate, 2007). Moreover, the culture of hyper-masculinity in the military tends to create an intolerance for deviation from traditional gender roles as well as promote strong sexism and heterosexism. Therefore, the presence of women and LGBT members in the military poses a threat to the manhood fundamental to the traditional masculine assumptions in the military (Dunivin, 1994). The systematic practice of sexism and heterosexism in the military is clearly demonstrated by the long history of exclusion policies towards women, lesbians, gays, and bisexuals, and the continuing practice of prohibiting transgender people from serving.

In the masculine culture of the military, women service members are required to demonstrate masculine/male/warrior qualities to be perceived as competent service members while dealing with gender stereotypes of women and sexist attitudes that negatively influence the evaluation of their competence and performance in the military. Therefore, their gender-minority status in the military creates a variety of challenges for women in the military. For instance, Herbert (1998), in her survey with approximately 300 women veterans, found: (a) 49% of the women experienced pressure to act feminine, masculine, or both in the military; and (b) 60% of the women believed that penalties exist for acting either too feminine or too masculine. Our participant, Angelina, talked about this too.

> There are three types of females in in the military. You can be a bitch, you can be a slut, or you can be a lesbian. These are your three choices. So you wanna be a bitch, but you don't want everyone to hate you. But if you start to be nice to people, they are going to think you are a slut. It's very hard. . .

To navigate the gender-related pressure and penalties in the military, 30% of the women in Herbert's study reported using a variety of strategies to appear and act more feminine, masculine, both, or neuter (minimizing both feminine and masculine qualities). A higher number of lesbians and bisexual women reported the use of gender management strategies compared to heterosexual women (19% as compared to 10%) (Herbert, 1998).

The effectiveness of gender management strategies seems to diminish when troops are deployed to war. In a recent study with 17 women Iraq War veterans, Demers (2013) also reported the use of gender management efforts among her participants as they "engaged in constant tension between being male enough to earn respect but not so male that they became a threat to their comrades" (p. 505). However, these women war veterans disclosed that the gender balance they cautiously crafted in the U.S. was disrupted once they were deployed to Iraq where they became "more warrior-like, that is, masculine" (p. 505).

113

Demers explained her findings as follows: "females' action became dire as male soldiers may have felt their masculinity threatened and responded by increasing their harassment of female veterans and turning against them, leaving the females to 'fight two wars'" (pp. 505–506). As a result of their gender-related experiences in the war zone, Demers' women participants experienced a loss of trust and a feeling of betrayal, while questioning their identity. Despite their effort to assimilate into the masculine culture, career advancement for women service members continues to be slower than that of males, and women remain underrepresented in the senior ranks of the military (Mulhall, 2009).

DISCRIMINATION IN THE MILITARY

Of the non-dominant groups in the military, because of "epidemic" rates of sexual harassment (Pryce et al., 2012, p. 12), White women are the most dissatisfied (Antecol & Cobb-Clark, 2009) while Black women "enjoy somewhat higher occupational prestige within the enlisted ranks" (Lundquist, 2008, p. 485). In their study of racial harassment and job satisfaction, Antecol and Cobb-Clark (2009) noted that environments intolerant of harassment have fewer incidences of harassment. Antecol and Cobb-Clark's data analysis revealed that racial discrimination in the military seems to be more about preferential treatment of in-group members than of unjust treatment of out-group members. They also characterized race relations as poor rather than positive. Those in more diverse work groups report less racial harassment. Antecol and Cobb-Clark found that the more positive the perception of equity in civilian life, the more dissatisfied military personnel of color were with military life. Though military personnel have potentially more opportunities to work in integrated settings than do civilians, they work in an environment with less protection from racial discrimination.

As the federal government requires institutions of higher education to do more to prevent and respond to sexual violence toward women, so too is the military under scrutiny to do the same. Though it is difficult to estimate the prevalence of sexual assault in the military, few question that it is substantial. According to the Service Women's Action Network (SWAN, 2014), approximately 20,000 sexual assaults occur in the military each year. Of those, only 13.5% to 14% are reported. Although combat experiences are the leading cause of PTSD in men, sexual assault is the primary cause of PTSD in women. Pryce et al. (2012) cited the definition of sexual assault from the Military Code of Uniform Justice, then lamented that what good is a definition if it is not enforced. They also acknowledged that though sexual assault and sexual harassment are societal problems, not only military ones, civilian prosecution is far more efficient. Estimates are that one in three women in the military are sexually assaulted, and that one in five on college campuses are sexually assaulted, although one in six women in the general civilian population are sexually assaulted (Kessler, 2014; O'Toole, 2012; Pryce et al., 2012). Kessler (2014) pointed out caution in these estimations. Such rates and their comparisons are often based on different questions or limited samples. Nonetheless, the likelihood of a woman being sexually assaulted in the U.S. is staggering and chances are greater for women in the military.

Societal views on women's roles certainly influence the rates of sexual assault and other experiences women endure in the military. U.S. views on the combat roles of women in the military have lagged behind those in Denmark, Belgium, Norway, Canada, Germany, Spain, and Israel (Kennedy & Malone, 2009). Yet, many women have noted the role of the military in creating opportunities that in civilian life were closed, such as aviation (Mohr, 2014). Lundquist (2008) cited Crosby's concept of the paradox of the female worker being more content than her male counterparts, especially in self-segregated work environments, regardless of discriminatory environments. Essentially, women appear to be grateful for the opportunity to work, regardless of the dangers from the enemy and comrades.

Women's health care is another source of discrimination. Women service members experience a lack of access and support for obtaining quality services to meet their unique health care needs (Mulhall, 2009). This was also described by our participant, Angelina, who told us about the term "pulling her V card." She said, "If a girl is going to complain that it's like that time of the month or she can't do this, people will say 'she is pulling her V card.' And you don't want to be that girl." In fact, women veterans consistently reported more reproductive and gynecological problems than civilian women (Rivera & Johnson, 2014). Also, women military service members reported higher rates of divorce and single parenthood than their male counterparts (Mulhall, 2009). These data indicate significant challenges for military women to maintain a balance between their family life and service (Mulhall, 2009).

In addition to sexism, the military has a long history of perpetuating heterosexist as well as antigay attitudes and behaviors despite the recent repeal of Don't Ask Don't Tell (DADT), on September 20, 2011 (Marshall, 2011). More equitable attitudes in U.S. society and in the military led to the change. However, before that change, approximately 14,500 service members were discharged between 1993 and 2011 because of DADT (Daniel, 2012). These service members who were discharged are not considered to be veterans by the VA; thus, they lost access to veteran benefits. Though bills in the House and Senate have been proposed that would restore benefits to these discharged service members, as of 2014 they are still in committee (Burke, 2014). Some of those discharged have been able to return to service, but the U.S. Defense Department does not keep such data. According to Daniel (2012) there have been some concerns reported about their return, but they have not been substantial.

Burks (2011) stated that the military has officially enforced heterosexuality as the dominant rule, and thousands of LGB persons have tried to hide their sexual orientation to maintain their military careers. For instance, RAND National Defense Research Institute's survey (2010) revealed that only 3% of LGB service members reported being open about their sexual orientation with others in their military units. Additionally, 46% of the LGB respondents reported that they avoid talking about sexual orientation, 22% pretend to be heterosexual, and 29% are selective about their sexual orientation disclosure (RAND National Defense Research Institute, 2010).

As evidenced by the above data, the majority of LGB service members have been forced to hide their sexual orientation in order to serve in the military. What are the costs of hiding a significant part of who they are? Unfortunately, sexual orientation concealment has major negative effects on LGB service members' health and well-being. Sexual orientation concealment is associated with minority group stress along with internalized homophobia and expectations of rejection (Meyer, 2003). In addition, minority group stress is related to clinical depression and psychological distress (Smith & Ingram, 2004). Moreover, concealing sexual orientation has a negative impact on developing social cohesiveness in the military. For example, in her study with 445 LGBT military veterans, Moradi (2009) found that sexual orientation concealment was negatively correlated with social cohesion, whereas sexual orientation disclosure was correlated significantly and positively with social strength. Also, Frank's (2004) qualitative study of 30 LGB service members serving in OEF and OIF also found that sexual orientation concealment hindered their relationships with their comrades; LGB service members who hid their sexual orientation in the military experienced a decline in morale, professional advancement, commitment, retention, and access to support services. These findings suggest social alienation among LGB service members, which is "particularly deleterious in military units in which interpersonal connection, support, and trust among unit members are thought to be paramount to unit cohesion and effectiveness" (Moradi, 2009, p. 515).

In our multi-site case study, one participant identified as being lesbian and was out to her unit and supervisor. Her experience was one of support. She lauded her supervisor for drawing out her leadership potential and believed she would not have considered attending graduate school without his encouragement. Yet, Daniel (2012) noted several examples of military members hiding their identity for decades, and those who continue to do so. The reluctance of military personnel to come out after years of disguise and fear of discovery is understandable, especially given the substantial amount of harassment and victimization experienced by LGB service members described below.

According to the annual reports by the OutServe-Servicemembers Legal Defense Network (SLDN), from 1994 to 2002 there were 3,716 reported incidents of antigay harassment including verbal abuse, physical abuse, and death threats toward LGB service members (OutServe-SLDN, 2003; Sobel, Wescott, Benecke, Osburn, & Cleghorn, 2000; Sobel, Cleghorn, & Osburn, 2001). Survey results from Balsam, Cochran, and Simpson (as cited in the American Psychological Association (APA) Joint Divisional Task Force on Sexual Orientation and Military Service, 2009) found that 36% of LGBT service members respondents were involved in sexual orientation investigations in the military, with more women than men (47.9% vs. 32.6%) reporting being investigated; 15% were physically isolated from their unit due to their sexual orientation; 12% were required to go through a psychiatric evaluation, 13% were threatened to be discharged if they did not "out" other LBGT service members; and 47.2% experienced verbal, physical, or sexual assault at least one time. Also, respondents of color reported a significantly higher rate of sexual orientation-related victimization in the military than their White counterparts (60.2% compared with 44.5%), and women reported more experience of sexual victimization compared to men (Balsam et al., as cited in APA, 2009). Furthermore, RAND National Defense Research Institute (2010) reported the following problems that LGB participants attributed to DADT: being at risk for blackmail or manipulation (91%); negative effects on personal relationships (86%); adverse unit bond (76%); stress and anxiety (72%); experience of mental health problems (35%); being teased or mocked (29%); and being threatened or injured by other service members (7%).

Repeal of DADT finally allowed LGB people to serve openly in the military. However, the military is still not a safe place for many LGB service members because there is a persistent culture of heterosexism in the military. In addition, the presence of openly LGB service members may heighten homophobia and discrimination (Johnson, Rosenstein, Buhrke, & Haldeman, 2013). In fact, Burks (2011) warned of the potential increase in harassment in the military due the increased visibility of gay and lesbian service members. Indeed, many LGB service members reported that they would take a "'wait and see' attitude" (p. 268) before changing their behaviors related to sexual-orientation disclosure after repeal of DADT (RAND National Defense Research Institute, 2010).

It is important to emphasize that the repeal of the DADT policy does *not* apply to transgender people. Indeed, "[t]he military has a binary view of gender; therefore, the rules and regulations including the language the military use reflect this view" (OutServe-SLDN, 2011, p. 27). Hence, the U.S. military continues to discriminate against transgender people by excluding anyone who identifies as or is suspected to be transgender. There are various medical, psychological, and criminal regulations that the military uses to disqualify transgender persons from serving in the military. For instance, any signs of genital surgery can disqualify an individual from serving (OutServe-SLDN, 2011). Also, the military considers transgender as a psychiatric disqualifying condition; thus, military criteria including "transsexualism," "transvestism," or "psychosexual condition" can be

117

applied to any person identifying as or suspected of being transgender (OutServe-SLDN, 2011, p. 29). These labels automatically eliminate a person from meeting the psychological fitness standard for military service. In addition, any individual exhibiting gender nonconforming dress or behaviors can be disciplined or persecuted for inappropriate or atypical conduct as these behaviors violate the military's binary view of gender (OutServe-SLDN, 2011). The U.S. military's policy toward transgender people is significantly behind compared to the following countries that allow transgender military services in some ways: Australia, Belgium, Canada, Czech Republic, Israel, Netherlands, Spain, Sweden, Thailand, and the United Kingdom (OutServe-SLDN, 2014).

Despite the U.S. military's transgender exclusion policies, many transgender people have served honorably and continue to serve in the military. In a survey with transgender military service members and veterans, Bryant and Schilt (2008) reported that 660 respondents identified themselves as transsexual, 97% of whom were not able to engage in gender transition until they separated from the military. Thirty-eight percent of the survey participants indicated that others assumed or questioned if they were gay, and 14% were asked by an officer about their sexual orientation, which was a violation of the DADT policy. A gender difference was also reported: transmen were suspected for being gay at a significantly higher rate than transwomen (72% as compared to 37%). The survey respondents also reported an organizational level of discrimination at Veterans Affairs Health Care, such as a lack of support for gender transition and disrespect from the VA medical staff. In response to the VA's discriminatory practices reported by transgender veterans, the Veterans Health Administration has recently issued a directive to all VA facilities to implement a policy to provide respectful health care service delivery to transgender and intersex veterans (U.S. Department of Veterans Affairs, 2013c). Although this is an important step in obtaining equal access for transgender veterans, the military continues to exclude transgender people from serving.

TRANSITION TO THE CIVILIAN WORLD

Transition from the military to civilian society is challenging for many veterans. However, research indicates that women veterans face more challenges than their male counterparts. First, despite the gender-related challenges described above, women in the military believe that their quality of life, financial compensation, and career advancement opportunities are significantly better in the military than in civilian society (Lundquist, 2008). Such perceptions held among military women may increase anxiety about their transition from the military. Nonetheless, higher rates of unemployment and homelessness are reported among women veterans compared with men (Mulhall, 2009). Thus, women veterans' anxiety about transition is understandable, especially since "women veterans have dramatically different employment experience than men" (Mulhall, 2009, p. 11).

Issues surrounding women veterans' identity are particularly challenging for them during their transition to civilian life. Despite the growing number of and contributions by women in the military, there continue to be strong stereotypes in society that women are not "real veterans" or that they are not exposed to "real danger" compared to male veterans (Street, Vogt, & Dutra, 2009). In our study, Angelina, a woman veteran who was deployed twice to a war zone, described the stereotypes as follows:

> Men are the ones who go and fight and that's what they [the public] think, so it's easier to walk up to a man and thank them. Females . . . I think they [the public] feel, we [females] can't deploy and could never be deployed. We [females] must sit behind a desk somewhere and take care of paperwork.

These stereotypes displayed by the general public make many women veterans like Angelina feel unsupported, invalidated, unappreciated, and "invisible." Angelina continued:

> I would rather be invisible as a civilian than as a soldier. Guys don't know what it's like not to feel thanked. They don't know that. They're the hero. We're like a fluke. Like a female in uniform is an oddity. It's an oddity. It's not the norm.

The constant dismissiveness of women military members' contributions could lead many women to internalize stereotypes. Indeed, many of them become "invisible" by not identifying themselves as veterans (Sander, 2012). A lack of veteran identity among women veterans makes their transition more difficult as they may not recognize that they are eligible for benefits and resources as a result of their military service (U.S. Department of Labor, 2011).

Another identity issue facing women veterans is their female gender identity. As described earlier, women in the military utilize gender management strategies in order to assimilate into the masculine culture. Although these strategies are an essential aspect for the development of women military service members, it can create complicated issues when they re-enter a civilian world that expects women to be more feminine than masculine. In her study with female Iraq War veterans, Demers (2013) states that "women veterans must struggle with what it means to be female in a society where civilians are perplexed by them and do not know whether to treat them 'like one of the guys . . . [or] like a lady'" (p. 505). This point was also shared by Angelina, a woman veteran in our study, as she noted civilians' anxiety: "I don't know if the public is kind of afraid of us. It could be . . . are they afraid of us?" Similarly, Wilmot (2013), a female veteran with combat experience, described her consistent encounters with civilian men who appeared intimidated by her combat experience. She wonders, "Is it that women serving in the military are quite threatening to a number of men because of the prescribed role women are 'expected' to serve in society?" (p. 76). These insights strongly suggest that women veterans' identity is significantly influenced by context, which makes their transition from the military to the civilian world complex.

Besides escaping from or dealing with discrimination, there are substantial physical and emotional effects of serving in the military. We turn to these now.

PSYCHOLOGICAL AND PHYSICAL EFFECTS

It is beyond the scope of this book to offer a thorough discussion of the psychological and physical effects of military service. Consequently, we provide only a brief discussion of those psychological and physical concerns that are reported most frequently by SVSM. It is important that higher education administrators, student affairs professionals, faculty, and staff realize that SVSM as a population are healthier than the general population (Shatuck & Brown, 2013). Cognitive and physical testing of recruits seeks to ensure that those who take the military oath are the healthiest of the general population. Nonetheless, according to Pryce et al. (2012), veterans bring their war home. What is it they are bringing home? Those in combat roles certainly risk greater physical and psychological repercussions of military service; however, those not in combat roles also risk ill effects. According to Kennedy and Malone (2009), women "are just as effective in managing stress in the military as men and in some cases may have an edge," however, "sexual trauma places women at significant risk of problems following wartime deployments" (p. 75). Unfortunately, such trauma occurs at every level of the military (Pryce et al., 2012).

In addition to sexual assault, popular and scholarly media highlight the ongoing concerns of PTSD, an anxiety disorder in which sufferers re-experience "distressing intrusive thoughts, dreams, reliving of the event, and psychological and physiological distress when exposed to cues" (Pryce et al., 2012, p. 35). In a meta-analysis, Richardson, Frueh, and Acierno, (2011) reported that studies found between 4% and 17% of U.S. Iraq War veterans have been diagnosed with PTSD, and 3% to 6% of U.K. Iraq War veterans have been diagnosed with PTSD. Moreover, the U.S. veteran prevalence of PTSD is two to four times more than the civilian population (Richardson et al., 2011). Pryce et al. (2012) wrote about other issues common to military personnel. These include overuse and misuse of alcohol and prescription drugs, soul wounds (profound questioning of identity and character), suicide, and sleep disorders. According to Mysliwiec et al. (2013) musculoskeletal injuries are the most frequently reported physical injuries, and PTSD, depression, anxiety, and traumatic brain injury (TBI) the most frequent psychological and neurological injuries. Sleep disorders are common in the military and not only for those in combat roles. Sleep disorders are increasingly diagnosed during and after deployments. Because of the ongoing shift work, 24-hour duty rotations, and the pressure to be tough and to not need sleep, sleep disorders such as short sleep disorder, insomnia, and sleep apnea are more prevalent than in civilian comparison groups (Mysliwiec et al., 2013; Shatuck & Brown, 2013). For example, 41.8% of veterans were found to suffer from short sleep disorder whereas only 9.3% of civilians report this problem. Furthermore, there is a strong correlation of pain syndrome with insomnia. It is important to realize that physical and emotional effects of military life are often co-diagnosed. Mysliwiec et al. (2012) found significant associations among PTSD, pain syndromes, and sleep disorders. Ghafoori and Hierholzer (2010) found level of combat exposure and level of PTSD symptoms appear to predict certain personality disorders. Using Williams and Berry's (1991) research, Ghafoori and Hierholzer hypothesized the increased levels of personality disorders of Latino veterans were due to acculturated stress, a concept we discussed in Chapter 2. Mysliwiec et al. argued that the co-diagnoses of physical and psychological concerns should be common sense. A soldier's lack of sleep increases the likelihood of accidents and keeps the body from the healing rest it needs. Relatedly, sleep disorder is a symptom of major depressive disorder which frequently occurs with PTSD. The most serious consequence of major depressive disorder is suicide (Pryce et al., 2012).

Suicide rates of veterans have been striking. According to Kemp and Bossarte (2012), of U.S. suicides from 1999 to 2011, approximately 22.2% were veterans. More appalling is that in 2010 approximately 22 veterans died from suicide every day. Kemp and Bossarte noted that in both the civilian and veteran populations, those who commit suicide are far more likely to be men. They and Pryce et al. (2012) wrote that those veterans who commit suicide tend to be older than 30 and half are experienced soldiers. For higher education, suicide is also a serious concern among SVSM on campus as a national survey revealed: 46% of SVSM indicated suicidal ideations, including 20% having a plan, 10.4% thinking frequently about suicide, 7.7% making an attempt, and 3.8% indicating suicide is "likely" or "very likely" (Rudd et al., 2011).

Concerns of the soul are those that "fundamentally reshape" basic values, which include what veterans believe and value (Pryce et al., 2012). These include judgments as integral to the self as notions of good and evil. This reshaping affects one's identity as well as relationships. How might the experiences of SVSM described in this chapter have an effect on their experience in higher education?

121

IMPLICATIONS AND RECOMMENDATIONS FOR HIGHER EDUCATION

Gender, race, and sexual orientation influence the experience of military service members and veterans. The military's strong culture of masculinity creates systematic organizational practices that produce discrimination, marginalization, and isolation, particularly for women, gays, lesbians, bisexuals, and transgender people. Therefore, it is essential to understand equity issues in the military so that student affairs professionals, higher education administrators, faculty, and staff can create a campus environment that is affirming, inclusive, and supportive for *all* SVSM regardless of race, gender, socioeconomic class, and sexual orientation.

To develop an inclusive environment for *all* SVSM, higher education leaders must foster a campus culture that does not tolerate sexism, racism, or hetero-sexism (Iverson & Anderson, 2013). It is critical for higher education leaders to recognize the role that the concept of masculinity plays within the higher education culture, structures, and practices as well as its implications for both SVSM and civilian students (Hamrick & Rumann, 2012). To this end, Iverson and Anderson (2013) recommended that universities provide educational oppor-tunities to critically examine the role of masculinity in the military as well as other social organizations (i.e. higher education). This could broaden campus members' understanding of the power dynamics embedded in various issues related to the military.

Further, when campus veteran services support SVSM by providing structures and camaraderie, it is essential not to perpetuate hyper-masculinity which can marginalize women and LBGT people (Hamrick & Rumann, 2012). Hamrick and Rumann (2012) also recommended that campus veterans services develop social and educational programs to increase awareness about the experiences of women in the military, and we believe that people of color and LGBT persons in the military should be included in this effort. Furthermore, veterans' services should employ diverse staff members and engage in active advocacy to promote the equality of all SVSM (Hamrick & Rumann, 2012).

Higher education administrators, student affairs professionals, faculty, and staff also need to understand the complexity of identities among women, people of color, and LGBT SVSM. For instance, as noted above, many women who served in the military do not identify themselves as veterans after they separate from the military (Sander, 2012). The lack of veteran identity among women was also apparent in our study as we struggled to obtain women SVSM participants. Moreover, when we asked men veterans about suggestions for names of women veterans we could interview, the men told us that the women veterans they knew were too busy. These men felt comfortable speaking for their female peers, perhaps seeing their role as these women's protectors. LGBT veterans who came out after separating from the military may experience high distress due to having been a member of an oppressed group (Iverson & Anderson, 2013; Meyer, 2003). Also, many transgender veterans start their gender transition after they leave the military. However, they may struggle with obtaining the necessary support and care for their transition. These examples suggest that it is more challenging for women and LGBT veterans to integrate their gender and/or sexual orientation identity. Therefore, it is vital for campus veterans services to collaborate with women's centers, multicultural student affairs offices, and LGBT support centers.

Campus health and counseling center staff must understand the influence of class, gender, race, and sexual orientation in SVSM's military experience, the intersection of these social identities with health and mental health issues, and how social identities of SVSM may influence their transition from military to civilian and college environments. To this end, it is essential for staff at health and counseling centers to stay current on military policies and practices that affect the lives of SVSM and seek professional consultation and legal resources when appropriate (Eleazer, 2013).

Regardless of what popular media may portray of college life, academic stress is an ubiquitous aspect of being a student. This is the case too for military combat-veterans (Shea & Fishback, 2012). Moreover, such stress can amplify equity issues, which include physical and psychological effects of military service and discrimination. All of these distract and even impair students from learning.

According to Christian et al. (2009), for those working with SVSM, providing an opportunity for SVSM to discuss their military history is beneficial, including the relationship they had with their units. Christian et al. also advise to look for evidence of isolation. This is often a warning sign of distress. Those leaving the military due to injury often feel guilty about having to leave their unit. To them it is an incomplete mission. Higher education administrators and student affairs professionals should not assume that being trained to kill is one of the most important aspects of the military training. It is not. Rather, teamwork to accomplish a mission is critical to meeting military goals.

Employees of institutions should be part of a trained network of professionals that extends off campus, who are familiar with the experiences of SVSM. This network should provide services but also be informed of military and VA support service options. This network must also be able to connect SVSM to needed resources even though this group is often reluctant to seek assistance (Shea & Fishback, 2012). In general, Shea and Fishback suggested that higher education administrators, student affairs professionals, faculty, and staff be patient with SVSM, understanding that they have unique and potentially harrowing experiences. SVSM deserve time to adjust to the campus climate and may need specific individual and group accommodations. Most importantly, higher education administrators and student affairs professionals must promote inclusion of SVSM into the campus, which adds perspective and life experience to both.

123

With the above equity issues in mind, how might inclusion be accomplished? Consider how it is for SVSM who come from not only a dangerous environment but also one in which there is work and private life integration beyond what is experienced in civilian life. SVSM may experience the campus as a segregated environment. As noted above, many women, and women and men of color, enter the military expecting more leadership responsibilities than are available in civilian life. Do they find this on campus?

Let's envision Pat whose story began this chapter as a former enlisted soldier of color now older than his college-aged undergraduate peers. He identified with his racially integrated unit. He now experiences the campus student veterans organization as a predominantly White group in a campus culture of subgroup expectations. He experiences the office of multicultural student affairs as predominately focused on the concerns of younger students. It is imperative that multicultural services and campus veterans services become close partners to accommodate the needs of older veterans of color who expect an integrated college environment.

What if Pat were a man and a combat soldier, as the research explored above? He would be more likely to struggle with PTSD, TBI, addictions, sleep disorders, flashbacks, have gained fewer skills in the military that translate to civilian life, and fewer family resources to assist him. Pryce et al. (2012) noted that "higher education is striving to cope effectively with returning veterans in the university environment, as TBI can cause functional impairments" (p. 38). What if Pat attended a community college with no counseling center? What too if Pat were a first-generation college student? How many combat SVSM are also first-generation students? Are they aware of resources that provide assistance? Are retention services for first-generation students accommodating for veterans? If not, is there a resource list of where services are available? What are the ethical issues of admitting and even recruiting students whose needs institutions cannot address?

If Pat were a woman, it is likely she would need a welcoming women's center. Does one exist? Does one exist that precludes a particular political point of view? Does the campus veterans' services office collaborate with the women's center to reach out to women SVSM who may be reluctant to identify as veterans? How are women SVSM welcomed to the campus student veterans' organization? Do they have a voice there? Are there any support groups specifically for women SVSM on campus? Whose role is it to ensure that inequity issues from the military do not permeate the campus? We believe that the director of campus veterans services and the advisor to the student veterans club should model equity not only in the welcoming of veterans to campus but also of women and LGBT veterans to veterans groups.

If Pat were gay or transgender, how might the campus LGBT center serve as a resource and source of strength for a working adult who has had to hide an important aspect of the self? What would it be like for Pat to be around a campus where being gay/transgender is likely to be more accepted than in the military? Would the LGBT community be patient, accommodating, and embracing of Pat's individuality? How do the LGBT center and campus veterans services office collaborate to support LGBT veterans' success in college?

If Pat were a person of color, proud of previous military leadership roles, how does the campus assist Pat in pursuing further more complex leadership opportunities? Are there opportunities available? How can those opportunities be found? Who assists Pat in finding them?

Campuses must consider not only the war Pat brings to campus but also Pat's social identities and equity experiences. How have these converged and evolved on the campus environment? Higher education administrators, student affairs professionals, faculty, and staff must consider how policy and practice can model patience and encourage individual and unique perspectives to create an environment conducive to learning and degree attainment, a goal similar for all students.

With the repeal of DADT and the combat restrictions for women, the military is (slowly) adapting to equity expectations that most institutions of higher education have embraced for some time. As we conclude our examination into SVSM and higher education, what might the future hold? What future trends are likely and what pending legislation might be instigated by such trends?

Chapter 8

Future Directions, Potential Challenges, and Conclusions

In this book we attempted to demonstrate the progress higher education has made in providing programs and services that address the unique needs and cultural characteristics of SVSM. We have also illuminated how higher education and the military can continue to improve programs and services for SVSM. With the projected return of troops from Afghanistan, will institutions continue their support of SVSM? If so, how will they? Who will be the advocates of SVSM and what will be the challenges for SVSM? Will legislation supporting SVSM continue to be a priority for policy makers or will they seek to decrease or cut educational programs? If, as we have advocated, SVSM are a diverse population worthy of special consideration, services to meet their unique circumstances should continue.

THE VA

As we write this final chapter, events surrounding the VA highlight systematic challenges for student veterans. Delayed backlogs in claims and benefits, long wait times to see physicians, and the alleged cover-up of waitlists that lead to veteran deaths, all contributed to former VA Secretary Eric Shinseki's resignation, prompting veterans and politicians to question the integrity of the VA. We hope that this increased attention and scrutiny of the VA will garner it the funding and political support that veterans deserve. Until then, other entities will need to fill service gaps caused by problems at the VA.

THE STUDENT VETERANS OF AMERICA (SVA)

A significant increase in the college SVSM population over the first decade of the 2000s led to a mass movement from non-profit organizations, higher education institutions, the VA, and federal and state governments to examine strategies for supporting SVSM as they transition from the military to the classroom. According to the SVA (2013a) over 1 million veterans have utilized the Post 9/11 GI Bill. The SVA has established key relationships with VA officials and other federal and state officials and while doing so the SVA has grown to over 1,000 local student veteran organizations nationwide. The SVA has become the national leader promoting key legislation such as in-state tuition rates for veterans and working with the VA and the National Student Clearing House to highlight the success rate of student veterans who have utilized the Post-9/11 GI Bill. We project that SVA will continue its lobbying efforts. Between 2013 and 2014 SVA has increased their staff substantially, worked with policy makers to push key legislation, developed numerous programs, and raised a substantial amount of support in corporate sponsorships from organizations such as Google and the Lumina Foundation. In 2013 through the Million Records Project (SVA, 2013c), SVA successfully diffused previous reports that lacked the methodology to demonstrate more accurate graduation rates of SVSM. SVA's comprehensive initial report released in 2014 showed that 51.7% of SVSM received a degree or certificate (Cate, 2014). Research such as this will be beneficial in highlighting the return on investment of the Post 9/11 GI Bill and other military educational programs. Continuing research at the state and national level by veteran service organizations, SVA, and higher education institutions will be necessary to make informed decisions about evolving innovative programs and services for SVSM.

PENDING LEGISLATION

Legislation involving veterans is dynamic, meaning numerous bills are being considered simultaneously. Resources we list in the Appendix contain websites that allow those who work with SVSM and those who want to advocate for them to be informed about pending federal legislation and its progress (i.e. who introduced it, how many times it has been read, whether it is in committee, and whether it was passed by either the House or Senate). In 2014 at the writing of this book pending legislation related to higher education includes requiring the VA to provide average time to process claims, streamlining the benefits approval processes, allowing admission application fees to be covered by VA education benefits, granting active duty status to Reservists with over 20 years of experience, and establishing a pilot program to reduce the shortage of VA psychiatrists. Probably the bills of greatest interest to readers are those that would allow SVSM nationwide to pay in-state tuition at public institutions. Because of the nature of military duty across the globe, it is difficult for SVSM to establish residency as required at many public institutions. Currently, 24 states have already passed such legislation including Ohio and Virginia. However, continual advocacy is needed because half of U.S. states have either pending or no in-state tuition legislation. As we explored the various levels of advocacy in Chapter 4, keeping informed about and advocating for or against legislation is an example of social/political advocacy. We suggest social and political advocacy, as discussed in Chapter 4, be used when public policy itself is causing difficulties in SVSM pursuing their education.

STATE INITIATIVES

Many states have worked independently of the federal government and each other to create programs and services and to craft policies that support SVSM. Hawaii, Arizona, Illinois, and Pennsylvania have created their own organizations aimed at supporting SVSM. These organizations provide a direct approach to garner support in individual states. For example, the Pennsylvania Student Veterans Coalition (PSVC) has worked extensively with state lawmakers to pass legislation such as priority class scheduling. In addition, the PSVC has collaborated with higher education institutions to grow the number of student veteran organizations to now over 50. Other states have advisory councils on military and veteran education. Student veteran advocates should push to establish more state-wide student veteran organizations and sustain existing ones. In addition to these groups working with legislatures, advocates could fill research gaps to educate key stakeholders on the challenges that SVSM often face as they transition from the military. However, the vast majority of states are without organizations like these. An alternative is for the VA to collaborate (if it can) with higher education institutions through their Vet Success Program which is aimed at assisting SVSM on campus. More likely, SVSM advocacy groups must continue working with the VA to push for more funding for schools to implement this program at both large and small institutions.

In providing support for SVSM, higher education has created opportunities to initiate new collaborations, advance research, and make important contributions to a variety of fields. For instance, significant developments have been made in the treatment of PTSD (e.g., research on PTSD, the training of clinicians, and new applications of mindfulness on veterans struggling with PTSD) as a result of increased collaboration among researchers and practitioners in higher education, the military, VA, and other organizations. Also, growing research on SVSM in the last decade has made valuable contributions to transition studies as well as advising of non-traditional adult students in higher education, but additional research is warranted.

FUTURE RESEARCH

Considerable research on SVSM has been conducted on the transition to higher education and the cultural differences between the military and higher education. More accurate data is now available about their graduation rates, but we do wonder about barriers for those SVSM who are not successful in their degree attainment. We hope that future research turns to how more specific charac-teristics of the military experience (e.g., branch, rate, and status—active duty or Guard/Reserve) influences SVSM learning outcomes. How too might type of institution attended influence SVSM degree attainment? We also believe the effects of military service and deployments on families and relationships is under-studied. Additional research on dual diagnoses of those SVSM with illnesses is certainly warranted. In considering the literature on the use of veteran educational benefits by social identity, we found there is a dearth of research about how American Indian veterans have used such benefits. We encourage researchers and funding agencies to pursue research of these topics.

DIVERSE STUDENT VETERAN LEADERSHIP

Larger campuses traditionally have a more robust SVSM population, thus they have a larger need for programs and services. Furthermore, these campuses typically have a greater diversity of SVSM including woman, people of color, LGBT, and others. A diverse and robust student veteran organization will better mirror the realities of the general population. It behooves institutions of higher education to encourage such diverse campus student veteran organizations. Moreover, it is key that higher education administrators and student affairs professionals assist student veteran organizations in finding SVSM leaders to advocate on behalf of their peers for years to come. If there are fewer SVSM enrolling into higher education, the probability of having students to be key leaders of these student veteran organizations at both large and small campuses may decrease. Yet, student veteran organizations at the University of Missouri and the University of Wisconsin-Madison have been active for a number of years. Thus, they can serve as models for other institutions on how to sustain SVSM advocacy efforts.

IMPLICATIONS OF POSSIBLE DRAWDOWNS

In considering the decrease of boots on the ground in the Global War on Terror, we have to examine what the SVSM population will look like in the future. First, we do not predict the SVSM population will decrease any time soon. In fact, the VA estimates an increase in SVSM enrollment by 20% over the next couple of years (ACE, 2013a). Hence, it will be important to continue to educate today's generation of veterans about their benefits as they leave the military. In cooperation with the U.S. Department of Defense, military branches have increased their efforts to educate service members about their benefits; this must persist. Second, even if the drawdown does occur, history informs us that young adults will be called upon in the future to serve their country and educational benefits will continue to be used as incentives. According to Stanley (2003), wars

129

disrupt the traditional educational route that many high school graduates take. Educational benefits for service members are intended to correct the disruption and allow veterans to achieve their educational goals (Stanley, 2003). Third, due to continued high unemployment, we predict high interest in educational benefits by future military recruits. The U.S. is recovering from the Great Recession of 2009, but the economic conditions facing the U.S. remain unfavorable in the public eye, with unemployment rates still hovering around 6 to 7% (Bureau of Labor Statistics, 2014). Because people with a college education have an advantage in the job market over those who do not, military service becomes a means for those with few resources to attend a higher education institution. This is especially true today with the Post 9/11 GI Bill paying tuition and fees to the school and SVSM receiving a housing allowance. It will be unfortunate and possible that military educational benefits may decrease and make additional institutional and personal resources necessary. SVSM advocacy groups must educate the public and higher education institutions about what SVSM bring to the classroom (i.e., their work, travel, culture, and leadership), and we strongly hope that higher education does not forget this lesson as well as the contributions that SVSM bring to higher education.

Several challenges could pose a threat to future service member enrollment. Due to current budget constraints, many service members are being forced to separate from the military early. Defense Secretary Chuck Hagel announced in 2014 that the Obama Administration would seek to shrink the U.S. Army to its smallest size since prior to World War II (Shanker & Cooper, 2014). As a result, this has led to military branches substantially reducing their recruitment efforts. According to the U.S. Navy Recruiting Command (n.d.), their recruitment efforts dropped from 40,112 in 2013 to 33,800 in 2014.

Although it is difficult to predict future enrollment of SVSM, a decrease in military personnel could lead to fewer veterans enrolling in higher education. Advancing research regarding the return on investment of educational programs such as the Post 9/11 GI Bill is warranted. Such research could also offer new and more complex insight into the nuanced challenges that SVSM and their families face when transitioning into college and how those challenges differ by social identities.

CONCLUSION

In essence higher education must increase its commitment to serving SVSM. Given the significant amount of self-advocacy conducted by SVSM of this generation, SVSM would not allow educational benefits or institution support to diminish for their subsequent generation peers, just like the previous generation of veterans supported this generation of SVSM. The military camaraderie continues as Stan, a director of campus veterans' services, witnessed:

We are lucky to have a group of veterans who came out of Vietnam and who said, "We are not going to let what happened to us happen to these guys and gals." So, I think we were finally able to separate the policy for the war from the person who was told to go fight the war.

It is time for higher education to separate out the politics surrounding student veterans and to continue supporting and truly honoring the experiences of those who have served their country. As illustrated throughout this book, the military experience of SVSM has a significant impact on higher education. For many, like Angelina, it changes them forever.

When you go to war, you are always at war for the rest of your life . . . My life . . . for the rest of my life, I am always going to remember what I went through and it's always at the back of my mind.

May educators remain dedicated to those who have been forever changed by serving their country.

References

Abes, E. S., Jones, S. R. & McEwen, M. K. (2007). Reconceptualizing the model of multiple dimensions of identity: The role of meaning-making capacity in the construction of multiple identities. *Journal of College Student Development*, *48*, 1–22.

(2014) *Advanced English Dictionary*. Retrieved from: http://worldnet.princeton.edu

Alexander, D. & Thelin, J. R. (2013). The military and higher education in the United States. In F. A. Hamrick & C. B. Rumann (Eds.), *Called to serve: A handbook on student veterans and higher education* (pp. 1–19). San Francisco, CA: Jossey-Bass.

American College Personnel Association (ACPA) and National Association of Student Personnel Administrators (NASPA). (2010). *Professional competency areas for student affairs practitioners*. Retrieved from: http://www.naspa.org/regions/regioniii/Professional%20Competency.pdf

American Council on Education (ACE). (2010a). *Accommodating student veterans with traumatic brain injury and post-traumatic stress disorder: Tips for campus faculty and staff*. Retrieved from: http://www.acenet.edu/news-room/Documents/Accommodating-Student-Veterans-with-Traumatic-Brain-Injury-and-Post-Traumatic-Stress-Disorder.pdf

American Council on Education (ACE). (2010b, May). *Veteran success jam: Ensuring success for returning veterans*. Retrieved from: http://www.acenet.edu/news-room/Documents/Ensuring-Success-for-Returning-Veterans.pdf

American Council on Education (ACE). (2012). *ACE to Enhance Online Toolkit Helping Institutions Serve Student Veterans*. Retrieved from: http://www.acenet.edu/news-room/Pages/Online-Toolkit-Serving-Veterans.aspx

American Council on Education (ACE). (2013a). *Toolkit for veteran friendly institutions*. Retrieved from: https://vetfriendlytoolkit.acenet.edu/create-a-successful-program/Pages/default.aspx

American Council on Education (ACE). (Producer). (2013b). *Using the joint services transcript to help build a bridge to success*. Webinar retrieved from: http://www.acenet.edu/news-room/Pages/Transcripts-for-Military-Personnel.aspx

American Psychological Association (APA) Joint Divisional Task Force on Sexual Orientation and Military Service. (2009). *Report of the Joint Divisional Task Force on Sexual Orientation and Military Services.* Retrieved from: http://www.apa.org/pi/lgbt/resources/19–44-taskforce-report.pdf

Antecol, H. & Cobb-Clark, D. (2009). Racial harassment, job satisfaction and intentions to remain in the military. *Journal of Popular Economies, 22*(3), 713–738, doi: 10.1007/s00148–007–0176–1

Arminio, J. & Grabosky, T. K. (2013). Promoting organizational change to create a veteran-friendly campus: A case study. In F. A. Hamrick & C. B. Rumann (Eds.), *Called to serve: A handbook on student veterans and higher education* (pp. 278–300). San Francisco, CA: Jossey-Bass.

Armstrong, P. (2014). *Bloom's taxonomy.* Retrieved from Vanderbilt University Center for Teaching website: http://cft.vanderbilt.edu/guides-sub-pages/blooms-taxonomy/

Baechtold, M. & DeSawal, D. M. (2009). Meeting the needs of women veterans. In R. Ackerman & D. DiRamio (Eds.), *Creating a veteran-friendly campus: Strategies for transition and success* (New Directions for Student Services, No. 126, pp. 35–44). San Francisco, CA: Jossey-Bass.

Bair, S. D. (2011). Making good on a promise: The education of Civil War orphans in Pennsylvania, 1863–1893. *History of Education Quarterly, 51,* 460–485, doi: 10.1111/j.1748–5959.2011.00354.x

Barón, P. M. (2014). *Perspectives of veterans in higher education: Exploring the term "student veteran" and the identity shifts between military and college* (Unpublished master's thesis). College Park, MD: University of Maryland.

Barrett, F. (1996). The organizational construction of hegemonic masculinity: The case of the U.S. Navy. *Gender, Work, and Organization, 3,* 129–142, doi: 10.1037/0022 3514.6.1173

Baum, E. & Stoller, E. (2014, March). *Questioning the gospel: Does searching for best practices harm the organization's health?* Workshop presented at the annual conference of the National Association of Student Personnel Administrators, Baltimore, MD.

Baxter Magolda, M. B. (2001). *Making their own way: Narratives for transforming higher education to promote self development.* Sterling, VA: Stylus.

Baxter Magolda, M. B. (2011). Commentary. In D. DiRamio & K. Jarvis (Eds.), *Veterans in higher education: When Johnny and Jane come marching to campus* (pp. 91–93). ASHE Higher Education Report, *37*(3). Hoboken, NJ: John Wiley & Sons.

Baxter Magolda, M. B. (2013). Foreword. In S. R. Jones & E. S. Abes, *Identity development of college students: Advancing frameworks for multiple dimensions of identity* (pp. xv–xviii). San Francisco, CA: Jossey-Bass.

Berry, J. W. (1980). Acculturation as varieties of adaptation. In A. Padilla (Ed.), *Acculturation: Theory, models, and findings* (pp. 9–25). Boulder, CO: Westview.

Berry, J. W. (2005). Acculturation: Living successfully in two cultures. *International Journal of Intercultural Relations, 29,* 697–712, doi: 10.1016/j.ijintrel.2005.07.013

Birgerstam, P. (2002). Intuition – the way to meaningful knowledge. *Studies in Higher Education, 27*, 431–444, doi: 10.1080/0307507022000011543

Black, T., Westwood, M. J. & Sorsdal, M. N. (2007). From the front line to the front of the class: Counseling students who are military veterans. In J. Lippincott & R. B. Lippincott (Eds.), *Special populations in college student counseling: A handbook for mental health professionals* (pp. 3–10). Alexandria, VA: American Counseling Association.

Blimling, G. S., Whitt, E. J. & Associates (1999). *Good practice in student affairs: Principles to foster student learning.* San Francisco, CA: Jossey-Bass.

Bonar, T. C. & Domenici, P. L. (2011). Counseling and connecting with the military undergraduate: The intersection of military service and university life. *Journal of College Student Psychotherapy, 25*, 204–219, doi: 10.1080/87568225.2011.581925

Boulton, M. (2007/2008). How the GI Bill failed African-American Vietnam war veterans. *The Journal of Blacks in Higher Education, 58*, 57–60. Retrieved from: http://jstor.org/stable/25073828

Bower, K. P. (2004). "A favored child of the state": Federal student aid at Ohio colleges and universities, 1934–1943. *History of Education Quarterly, 44*, 364–387, doi: 10.1111/j.1748–5959.2004.tb00014.x

Branker, C. (2009). Deserving design: The new generation of student veterans. *Journal of Postsecondary Education and Disability, 21*(1), 59–66.

Brooks, G. R. (2001). Counseling and psychotherapy with male military veterans. In G. R. Brooks & G. E. Good (Eds.), *The new handbook of psychotherapy and counseling with men: A comprehensive guide to settings, problems, and treatment approaches* (Vol. 1, pp. 206–226). San Francisco, CA: Jossey-Bass.

Brown, G. (1988). Transsexuals in the military: Flight into hypermasculinity. *Archives of Sexual Behavior, 17*, 527–537.

Bryant, K. & Schilt, K. (2008). *Transgender people in the U.S. military: Summary and analysis of the 2008 Transgender American Veterans Association study.* Retrieved from University of California, Santa Barbara, Palm Center website: http://www.palmcenter.org/system/files/TGPeopleUSMilitary.pdf

Bureau of Labor Statistics (2014, June 6). *Employment situation summary.* Retrieved from: http://www.bls.gov/news.release/empsit.nr0.htm

Burke, M. M. (2014, February 12). Senate bill would provide clean service records for discharged gay, lesbian troops. *Stars and Stripes.* Retrieved from: http://www.stripes.com/senate-bill-would-provide-clean-service-records-for-discharged-gay-lesbian-troops-1.267291

Burks, D. J. (2011). Lesbian, gay, and bisexual victimization in the military: An unintended consequence of "Don't Ask, Don't Tell"? *American Psychologist, 66*, 604–613, doi: 10.1037/a0024609

Burnett, S. E. & Segoria, J. (2009). Collaboration for military transition students from combat to college: It takes a community. *Journal of Postsecondary Education and Disability, 22*(1), 53–58.

Busher, E. J. (1996). *Professional ethics: An investigation of student affairs professionals' compliance with the American College Personnel Association's statement of ethical principles and standards* (Doctoral dissertation). Retrieved from ProQuest Dissertations and Theses (UMI No. 9636515).

Cate, C. A. (2014). *Million Records Project: Research from Student Veterans of America*. Retrieved from Student Veterans of America website: http://www.studentveterans.org/what-we-do/million-records-project.html#data

Center for Collegiate Mental Health. (2013). *Annual report*. Retrieved from: http://ccmh.squarespace.com/storage/2013_CCMH_Report.pdf

Center for Universal Design. (1997). *The principles of university design, version 2.0*. Retrieved from: http://www.ncsu.edu/www/ncsu/design/sod5/cud/about_ud/udprinciplestext.htm

Chang, M. J. (2002). The impact of an undergraduate diversity course requirement on students' racial views and attitudes. *Journal of General Education, 51*, 21–42, doi: 10.1353/jge.2002.0002

Chickering, A. & Gamson, Z. F. (1987). *Seven principles for good practice in undergraduate education*. Retrieved from University of North Carolina Charlotte, Center for Teaching and Learning website: http://teaching.uncc.edu/articles-books/best-practice-articles/instructional-methods/7-principles

Chickering, A. W. & Reisser, L. (1993). *Education and identity* (2nd ed.). San Francisco, CA: Jossey-Bass.

Childress, J. & Childress, T. L. (2011, November 1). *Assessing needs of student veterans at an urban commuter institution*. Retrieved from Indiana University, Purdue University at Indianapolis University College, Office of Research, Planning and Evaluation website: www.planning.iupui.edu/567.html

Christian, J. R., Stivers, J. R. & Sammons, M. T. (2009). Training to the warrior ethos: Implications for clinicians treating military members and their families. In R. S. Morgillo, B. A. Moore & A. Freeman (Eds.), *Living and surviving in harm's way: A psychological treatment handbook for pre- and post- deployment of military personnel* (pp. 27–49). Hoboken, NJ: Routledge.

Clemens, E. V. & Milson, A. S. (2008). Enlisting service members' transition into the civilian world of work: A cognitive information processing approach. *The Career Development Quarterly, 56*, 246–256.

Costa, D. L. (1995). Pensions and retirement: Evidence from Union Army veterans. *The Quarterly Journal of Economics, 110*, 297–319.

Council for the Advancement of Standards in Higher Education (CAS). (2012). *CAS professional standards for higher education* (8th ed.). Washington, DC: CAS.

Creswell, J. W. (2013). *Qualitative inquiry and research design: Choosing among five approaches* (3rd ed.). Los Angeles, CA: Sage.

Crotty, M. (1998). *The foundations of social research: Meaning and perspective in the research process.* Thousand Oaks, CA: Sage.

135

Daniel, L. (2012, June 20). Nine months after repeal, gay troops slowly come out. *American Forces Press Service*. Retrieved from U.S. Defense Department website: http://www.defense.gov/news/newsarticle.aspx?id=116825

Dean, E. T. (1992). The myth of the troubled and scorned Vietnam veteran. *Journal of American Studies, 26*(1), 59–74. Retrieved from: http://www.jstor.org/stable/27555590

Deanna, L. A. (2001). *A voice for students: The advocacy role of student affairs professionals in higher education* (Doctoral dissertation). Retrieved from ProQuest Dissertations and Theses (UMI No. 3015505).

Dean of Students Office (2011). *Veterans assistance*. Retrieved from: http://students.wisc.edu/doso/vetsassistance.html

Demers, A. L. (2013). From death to life: Female veterans, identity negotiation, and reintegration into society. *Journal of Humanistic Psychology, 53*, 489–515, doi: 10.1177/0022167812472395

DeSawal, D. M. (2013). Contemporary student veterans and service members: Enrollment patterns and student engagement. In F. A. Hamrick & C. B. Rumann (Eds.), *Called to serve: A handbook on student veterans and higher education* (pp. 71–86). San Francisco, CA: Jossey-Bass.

DiRamio, D. & Jarvis, K. (2011). *Veterans in higher education: When Johnny and Jane came marching to campus*. ASHE Higher Education Report, *37*(3). Hoboken, NJ: Wiley & Sons.

Dortch, C. (2012, October 12). *GI bills enacted prior to 2008 and related veterans' educational assistance programs: A primer* (Congressional Report no. R42785). Washington, DC: Library of Congress Congressional Research Service. Retrieved from: http://www.fas.org/sgp/crs/misc/R42785.pdf

Downs, D. A. (2009, May 15). ROTC and the future of liberal education. *The Chronicle of Higher Education*, p. B8. Retrieved from: http://chronicle.com/article/ROTCthe-Future-of-Liberal/44356/

Dunivin, K. O. (1994). Military culture: Change and continuity. *Armed Forces & Society, 20*, 531–547.

Dykman, M. M. (2013). *UNM veterans resource center: Developing a veteran focused campus*. Retrieved from: http://www.nmlegis.gov/lcs/handouts/MVAC%20070113%20Item%205%20Veterans%20Resource%20Center%20Handout%201.pdf

Eisenhart, R. W. (1998). You can't hack it, little girl: A discussion of the covert psychological agenda of modern combat training. In P. Karsten (Ed.), *The training and socializing of military personnel* (pp. 209–219). New York, NY: Garland.

Eleazer, J. (2013, June). *Ethical considerations for medical and mental health professionals working with Trans* military service members*. Paper presented at the meeting of Trans Health Conference, Philadelphia, PA.

Erhrenreich, B. (1997). *Blood rites*. New York, NY: Metropolitan Books.

Exum, H. A., Coll, J. E. & Weiss, E. L. (2011). *A civilian counselor's primer for counseling veterans* (2nd ed.). Deer Park, NY: Linus.

Field, K. (2004, December 10). Court upholds colleges' ban on recruiters for military. *The Chronicle of Higher Education*, p. A1. Retrieved from: chronicle.com/article/Court-Upholds-Colleges-Bans/4465/

First Morrill Act, Ch. 130, 12 Stat. 503, 7 U.S.C. 301 et seq. (1862).

Francis, L. C. & Kraus, A. (2012, September–October). Developing a veterans center: The confluence of academic and military culture. *About Campus*, 11–14, doi: 10.1002/abc.2108759

Frank, N. (2004). *Gays and lesbians at war: Military service in Iraq and Afghanistan under "Don't Ask, Don't Tell."* Santa Barbara, CA: University of California Santa Barbara, Center for the Study of Sexual Minorities in the Military.

Frankel, R., Swanson, S. R. & Sagan, M. (2005). The role of individualism/collectivism classroom encounters: A four country study. *Journal of Teaching in International Business*, *17*, 33–59, doi: 10.1300/J066v17n01_03

Gasman, M. (2007). *Envisioning Black colleges: A history of the United Negro college fund.* Baltimore, MD: Johns Hopkins University Press.

Gates, G. J. (2004). *Gay men and lesbians in the U.S. military: Estimates from Census 2000.* Retrieved from the Urban Institute website: http://www.urban.org/Uploaded PDF/411069_GayLesbianMilitary.pdf

Gates, G. (2010). *Lesbian, gay, and bisexual men and women in the US military: Updated estimates.* Retrieved from the Williams Institute website: http://williamsinstitute.law.ucla.edu/wp-content/uploads/Gates-GLBmilitaryUpdate-May-20101.pdf

Ghafoori, B. & Hierholzer, R. W. (2010). Personality patterns among Black, White, and Hispanic combat veterans. *Psychological Trauma: Theory, Practice, and Policy*, *2*(1), 12–18, doi: 10.1037/a0019019

Glesne, C. (2011). *Becoming qualitative* (4th ed.). New York, NY: Longman.

Green, G., Emslie, C., O'Neill, D., Hunt, K. & Walker, S. (2010). Exploring the ambiguities of "masculinity" in accounts of emotional distress in the military among young ex-servicemen. *Social Science & Medicine*, *71*, 1480–1488, doi: 10.1016/j.socscimed.2010.07.015

Griffith, K. & Gilbert, C. (2012). *Easing the transition from combat to classroom: Preserving America's investment in higher education for military veterans through institutional assessment.* Retrieved from Center for American Progress website: http://www.americanprogress.org/wp-content/uploads/issues/2012/04/pdf/student_veterans.pdf

Hamrick, F. A. & Rumann, C. B. (2012, Spring). Addressing the needs of women service members and veterans in higher education. *On Campus with Women*, *40*, 4–5.

Harada, H. D., Damron-Rodriguez, J., Villa, V. M., Washington, D. L., Dhanani, S., Shon, H., Chattopadhyay, M., Fishbein, H., Lee, M., Makinodan, T. & Andersen, R. (2002). *Veteran identity and race/ethnicity: Influence on VA outpatient care utilization.* Retrieved from National Center for Biotechnology Information website: http://www.ncbi.nlm.nih.gov/pubmed/11789624

137

Harper, S. R. & Quaye, S. J. (2009). Beyond sameness, with engagement and outcomes for all. In S. R. Harper & S. J. Quaye (Eds.), *Student engagement in higher education: Theoretical perspectives and practical approaches for diverse populations* (pp. 1–15). New York, NY: Routledge.

Harrison, L. M. (2010). Consequences and strategies student affairs professionals engage in their advocacy roles. *Journal of Student Affairs Research and Practice, 47,* 197–214, doi: 10.2202/1949–6605.6003

Hassan, A. M., Jackson, R. J., Lindsay, D. R., McCabe, D. G. & Sanders, III, J. E. (2010, May–June). The veteran student in 2010. *About Campus, 15,* 30–32, doi: 10.1002/abc.20020

Helms, J. (Ed.) (1990). *Black and White racial identity: Theory, research, and practice.* Westport: CT: Greenwood Press.

Herbert, M. S. (1998). *Camouflage isn't only for combat: Gender, sexuality, and women in the military.* New York, NY: New York University Press.

Higate, P. R. (2007). Peace keepers, masculinities, and sexual exploitation. *Men and Masculinities, 10,* 99–119, doi: 10.1177/1097184X06291896

Hofstede, H. (2001). *Culture's consequences* (2nd ed.). Thousand Oaks, CA: Sage.

Holt, S. A. (2002, May). Why George Washington let the Army starve: Necessity meets democracy at Valley Forge. *Pennsylvania Legacies, 2*(1), 6–10, 12. Retrieved from: http://www.jstor.org/stable/27764822

Huckabee, C. (2011, March 3). Harvard to welcome Naval ROTC back to campus. *The Chronicle of Higher Education.* Retrieved from: http://chronicle.com/blogs/ticker/harvard-to-welcome-naval-rotc-back-to-campus/31030 http://chronicle.com/blogs/ticker/harvard-to-welcome-naval-rotc-back-to-campus/31030

Humes, E. (2006). How the GI Bill shunted blacks into vocational training. *The Journal of Blacks in Higher Education, 53,* 92–104. Retrieved from: http://www.jstor.org/stable/25073543

Illinois General Assembly. (2009, August 7). *Higher Education Veterans Service Act.* Retrieved from: http://www.ilga.gov/legislation/ilcs/ilcs3.asp?ActID=3112&ChapterID=18

Iverson, S. V. & Anderson, R. (2013). The complexity of veteran identity: Understanding the role of gender, race, and sexuality. In F. A. Hamrick & C. R. Rumann (Eds.), *Called to serve: A handbook on student veterans and higher education* (pp. 89–113). San Francisco, CA: Jossey-Bass.

Jackson, Jr., T., Fey, C. J. & Ross, L. E. (2013). Institutional leadership on serving student veterans and service members. In F. A. Hamrick & C. B. Rumann (Eds.), *Called to serve: A handbook on student veterans and higher education* (pp. 255–275). San Francisco, CA: Jossey-Bass.

Johnson, W. B., Rosenstein, J. E., Buhrke, R. A. & Haldeman, D. C. (2013, November 11). After "Don't Ask Don't Tell": Competent care of lesbian, gay and bisexual military personnel during the DoD Policy Transition. *Professional Psychology: Research and Practice.* Advance Online Publication, doi: 10.1037/a0033051

Jones, S. R. & Abes, E. S. (2013). *Identity development of college students: Advancing frameworks for multiple dimensions of identity*. San Francisco, CA: Jossey-Bass.

Jones, S. R. & McEwen, M. K. (2000). A conceptual model of multiple dimensions of identity. *Journal of College Student Development*, *41*, 405–413.

Josselson, R. (1987). *Finding herself: Pathways to identity development in women*. San Francisco, CA: Jossey-Bass.

Keene, J. D. (2001). *Doughboys, the Great War, and the remaking of America*. Baltimore, MD: Johns Hopkins University Press.

Kegan, R. (1994). *In over our heads: The mental demands of modern life*. Cambridge, MA: Harvard University Press.

Kemp, J. & Bossarte, R. (2012). *Suicide data report, 2012: Department of Veterans Affairs mental health services suicide prevention program*. Retrieved from U.S. Veterans Affairs website: http://www.va.gov/opa/docs/suicide-data-report-2012-final.pdf

Kennedy, C. H. & Malone, B. A. (2009). Integration of women into the modern military. In S. M. Freeman, B. A. Moore & A. Freeman (Eds.), *Living and surviving in harm's way* (pp. 67–84). New York, NY: Routledge.

Kessler, G. (2014, May 1). One in five women sexually assaulted: The source of the statistic. *Washington Post*. Retrieved from: http://www.washingtonpost.com/blogs/fact-checker/wp/2014/05/01/one-in-five-women-in-college-sexually-assaulted-the-source-of-this-statistic/

Kognito Interactive (Producer). (2013). *Supporting veterans on campus* [Webinar]. Retrieved from: http://vimeo.com/37744516

Kraus, A. & Rattray, N. A. (2013). Understanding disability in the student veteran community. In F. A. Hamrick & C. B. Rumann (Eds.), *Called to serve: A handbook on student veterans and higher education* (pp. 116–137). San Francisco, CA: Jossey-Bass.

Kroth, M. & Boverie, P. (2000). Life mission and adult learning. *Adult Education Quarterly*, *50*, 134–149. Retrieved from: aeq.sagepub.com

Krueger, G. (2000). Military culture. *Encyclopedia of Psychology*, *5*, 252–259.

Kuh, G. D., Kinzie, J., Schuh, J. H. & Whitt, E. J. (2010). *Student success in college*. San Francisco, CA: Jossey-Bass.

Lair, M. H. (2011). *Armed with abundance: Consumerism and soldiering in the Vietnam War*. Chapel Hill: University of North Carolina Press.

Lang, J. (2012). The life of a student veteran on a college campus: A student veteran perspective. *HigherEd Jobs*. Retrieved from: http://www.higheredjobs.com/articles/articleDisplay.cfm?ID=391

Lang, J. (2013). Vignette. In F. A. Hamrick & C. B. Rumann (Eds.), *Called to serve: A handbook on student veterans and higher education* (pp. 39–40). San Francisco, CA: Jossey-Bass.

Lee, C. C. & Rodgers, R. A. (2009). Counselor advocacy affecting systemic change in the public arena. *Journal of Counseling & Development*, *87*, 284–287.

139

Lewis, J. A., Lewis, M. D., Daniels, J. A. & D'Andrea, M. J. (1998). *Community counseling: Empowerment strategies for a diverse society* (2nd ed.). Pacific Grove, CA: Brooks/Cole.

Lewis, J. A., Arnold, M. S., House, R. & Toporek, R. L. (2002). *ACA advocacy competencies.* Retrieved from the American Counseling Association website: http://www.counseling.org/Resources/Competencies/Advocacy_Competencies.pdf

Livingston, W. G., Havice, P. A., Cawthon, T. W. & Fleming, D. S. (2011). Coming home: Student veterans' articulation of college re-enrollment. *Journal of Student Affairs Research and Practice, 48,* 315–331, doi: 10.2202/1949–6605.6292

Livingston, W. G., Scott, D. A., Havice, P. A. & Cawthon, T. W. (2012). Social camouflage: Interpreting male student veterans' behavior for residence life professionals. *The Journal of College and University Student Housing, 39*(1), 177–185.

Lopez-Baez, S. I. & Paylo, M. J. (2009). Social justice advocacy: Community collaboration and systems advocacy. *Journal of Counseling & Development, 87,* 276–283.

Lundquist, J. H. (2008). Ethnic and gender satisfaction in the military: The effect of a meritocratic institution. *American Sociological Review, 73,* 477–496.

McBain, L., Kim, Y. M., Cook, B. J. & Snead, K. M. (2012). *From solder to student II: Assessing campus programs for veterans and service members.* Retrieved from American Council on Education website: http://www.acenet.edu/news-room/Documents/From-Soldier-to-Student-II-Assessing-Campus-Programs.pdf

McCormack, B. (2009). The problem with problem solving. *Issues in Integrative Studies, 27,* 17–34. Retrieved from: http://www.units.muohio.edu/aisorg/pubs/issues/toclist.shtml

McDuffie, E. & Brown, G. R. (2010). 70 U.S. veterans with gender identity disturbances: A descriptive study. *International Journal of Transgenderism, 12,* 21–30, doi: 10.1080/15532731003688962

McGurk, D., Cotting, D. I., Britt, T. W. & Adler, A. B. (2006). Joining the ranks: The role of indoctrination in transforming civilians to service members. In T. W. Britt, A. B. Adler & C. A. Castro (Eds.), *Military life: The psychology of service in peace and combat: Vol. 2. Operational stress* (pp. 13–31). Westport, CT: Praeger.

MacLean, A. & Parsons, N. L. (2010). Unequal risk: Combat occupations in the volunteer military. *Sociological Perspectives, 53,* 347–372, doi: 10.1525/sop.2010.53.3.347

Marshall, C. & Rossman, G. B. (2011). *Designing qualitative research* (5th ed.). Thousand Oaks, CA: Sage.

Marshall, Jr., T. C. (2011, September 20). *Defense leaders laud repeal, return of "equality."* Retrieved from U.S. Department of Defense website: http://www.defense.gov/home/features/2010/0610_dadt/

Merriam, S. (2009). *Qualitative research: A guide to design and implementation* (rev. ed.). San Francisco, CA: Jossey-Bass.

Meyer, I. H. (2003). Prejudice, social stress, and mental health in lesbian, gay, and bisexual populations: Conceptual issues and research evidence. *Psychological Bulletin, 129,* 674–697.

Milem, J., Chang, M. J. & Antonio, A. L. (2005). Making diversity work on campus: A research-based perspective. Washington, DC: Association of American Colleges and Universities. Retrieved from: http://www.aacu.org/inclusive_excellence/documents/Milem_et_al.pdf

Military Family Research Institute at Purdue University and Student Veterans of America (SVA). (2013). *Success in 3-D for student veterans: How to design, develop and deliver a thriving SVO* (2nd ed.). Retrieved from: http://studentveterans.org/images/Documents/SucessIn3D-2013.pdf

Mizzou Student Veterans Association. (2013). *Eagles and anchors research*. Retrieved from: http://msva.students.missouri.edu/history/eagles-and-anchors-research/

Mohr, M. (2014, March). The sky is the limit. Retrieved from: USairwaysmag.com

Moradi, B. (2009). Sexual orientation disclosure, concealment, harassment, and military cohesion: Perceptions of LGBT military veterans. *Military Psychology, 21,* 513–533, doi: 10.1080/08995600903206453

Mosch, T. R. (1971, January). Updated veterans educational benefits. *Phi Delta Kappan, 52,* 280–282. Retrieved from: http://www.jstor.org/stable/20372873

Mulhall, E. (2009). *Women warriors: Supporting she "who has borne the battle."* Retrieved from Iraq and Afghanistan Veterans of America website: http://media.iava.org/IAVA_WomensReport_2009.pdf

Mysliwiec, V., McGraw, L. Pierce, R., Smith, P., Trapp, B. & Roth, B. J. (2013). Sleep disorders and associated medical comorbidities in active duty military personnel, *Sleep, 36,* 167–174. Retrieved from: http://dx.doi.org/10.5665/sleep.2364

National Association of Independent Colleges and Universities. (2007). *Introductory statement of Senator James Webb (D-VA) to the "Post-9/11 Veterans Educational Assistance Act of 2007."* Retrieved from: http://www.naicu.edu/special_initiatives/gibill/publications/page/introductory-statement-of-senator-james-webb-d-va-to-the-post-911-veterans-educational-assistance-act-of-2007

Nichols-Casebolt, A. (2012, March–April). The green zone: A program to support military students on campus. *About Campus,* 26–29, doi: 10.1002.abc.21070.

Oberly, J. W. (1985). Gray-haired lobbyists: War of 1812 veterans and the politics of bounty land grants. *Journal of the Early Republic, 5*(1), 35–58, doi: 10.2307/3122504

Ohio University. (2013). *Application for admission and scholarships.* Retrieved from: http://www.ohio.edu/admissions/forms/upload/domestic_form_withHTC_14–15_final-2.pdf

O'Neil, S. (2013, July 8). *Earn while you learn: VA's work–study program.* Retrieved from Vantage Point website: http://www.blogs.va.gov/VAntage/9779/earn-while-you-learn-vas-work-study-program/

Ortiz, S. R. (2006). The "new deal" for veterans: The Economy Act, the Veterans of Foreign Wars, and the origins of New Deal dissent. *Journal of Military History, 70,* 415–438. Retrieved from: http://jstor.org/stable/4137959

O'Toole, M. (2012, October 6). Military sexual assault epidemic continues to claim victims as Defense Department fails females. *Huffington Post.* Retrieved from: http://www.huffingtonpost.com/2012/10/06/military-sexual-assault-defense-department_n_1834196.html

OutServe-Servicemembers Legal Defense Network (SLDN). (2003). *Unbecoming: The ninth annual report on "don't ask, don't tell, don't pursue, don't harass."* Retrieved from: http://sldn.3cdn.net/d7e44bb7ad24887854_w6m6b4y13.pdf

OutServe-Servicemembers Legal Defense Network (SLDN). (2011). *Freedom to serve: The definitive guide to LGBT military service.* Retrieved from: http://sldn.3cdn.net/5d4dd958a62981cff8_v5m6bw1gx.pdf

OutServe-Servicemembers Legal Defense Network (SLDN). (2014). *Transgender military service.* Retrieved from: http://www.sldn.org/pages/transgender-issues

Parrish, K. (2013). *VA announces big expansion of "VetSuccess on Campus."* Retrieved from Armed Forces Press Service website: http://www.defense.gov/news/news article.aspx?id=120692

Pat Tillman Foundation. (2014). *Who we are.* Retrieved from: http://pattillman foundation.org/

Pellegrin, J. (2013, January/February). The veteran's view. *About Campus,* 16–21, doi: 10.1002/abc.21101

Pennsylvania Student Veterans Coalition. (2013). *Mission and vision.* Retrieved from: http://www.pasvc.org/mission—vision.html

Perry, W. G. Jr. (1981). Cognitive and ethical growth: The making of meaning. In A. W. Chickering (Ed.), *The modern American college* (pp. 76–116). San Francisco, CA: Jossey-Bass.

Persyn, J. M. & Polson, C. J. (2012). Evolution and influence of military adult education. In J. Zacharakis & C. J. Polson (Eds.), *Beyond training: The rise of adult education in the military* (New Directions for Adult and Continuing Education, No. 136, pp. 5–16). San Francisco, CA: Jossey-Bass.

Pope, R. L. & LePeau, L. (2012). The influence of institutional context and culture. In J. Arminio, V. Torres & R. L. Pope (Eds.), *Why aren't we there yet? Taking personal responsibility for creating an inclusive campus* (pp. 103–130). Sterling, VA: Stylus.

Pope, R. L. & Reynolds, A. L. (1997). Student affairs core competencies: Integrating multicultural awareness, knowledge, and skills. *Journal of College Student Development, 38,* 266–275.

Pope, R. L., Reynolds, A. L. & Mueller, J. A. (2004). *Multicultural competence in student affairs.* San Francisco, CA: Jossey-Bass.

Pryce, J. G., Pryce, D. H. & Shackelford, K. K. (2012). *The costs of courage: Combat stress, warriors, and family survival.* Chicago, IL: Lyceum Books.

Quizon, D. (2011, April 22). After 42 years, Columbia will reinstate Naval ROTC. *The Chronicle of Higher Education.* Retrieved from: http://chronicle.com/blogs/ticker/after-42-years-columbia-u-will-reinstate-naval-rotc/32388

Raimundo, A. (2010). The Filipino veterans equity movement: A case study in reparations theory. *California Law Review*, *98*, 575–623. Retrieved from: http://jstor.org/stable/20743980

RAND National Defense Research Institute. (2010). *Sexual orientation and U.S. military personnel policy: An update of RAND 1993 Study*. Retrieved from: http://www.rand.org/content/dam/rand/pubs/monographs/2010/RAND_MG1056.pdf

Ratts, M. J., Toporek, R. L. & Lewis, J. A. (2010). *ACA advocacy competencies: A social justice framework for counselors*. Alexandria, VA: American Counseling Association.

Reinhardt, C. & Ganzel, B. (2013). *The GI bill*. Retrieved from: http://www.livinghistoryfarm.org/farminginthe40s/life_20.html

Reisser, L. (2011). Commentary. In D. DiRamio & K. Jarvis, *Veterans in higher education: When Johnny and Jane came marching to campus* (p. 67). ASHE Higher Education Report, *37*(3). Hoboken, NJ: Wiley & Sons.

Resch, J. P. (1982). Welfare for revolutionary war veterans. *Social Service Review*, *56*, 171–195. Retrieved from: http://jstor.org/stable60000115

Richardson, L. K., Frueh, C. B. & Acierno, R. (2011). *Prevalence estimates of combat-related PTSD: A critical review*. Retrieved from National Center for Biotechnology Information website: http://www.ncbi.nlm.nih.gov/pmc/articles/PMC2891773/

Rivera, J. C. & Johnson, A. E. (2014). Female veterans of Operations Enduring and Iraqi Freedom: Status and future directions. *Military Medicine*, *179*, 133–136.

Rudd, M. D., Goulding, J. & Bryan, C. J. (2011). Student veterans: A national survey exploring psychological symptoms and suicide risk. *Professional Psychology: Research and Practice*, *42*, 354–360, doi: 10.1037/a0025164.

Rueb, J. D., Erskine, H. J. & Foti, R. J. (2008). Intelligence, dominance, masculinity, and self monitoring: Predicting leadership emergence in a military setting. *Military Psychology*, *20*, 237–252.

Rumann, C. B. & Hamrick, F. A. (2010). Student veterans in transition: Re-enrolling after war-zone deployments. *Journal of Higher Education*, *8*, 431–458, doi: 10.1353/jhe.0.0103.

Sander, L. (2012, July 30). Female veterans on campuses can be hard to spot, and to help. *Chronicle of Higher Education*, *58*(42), pp. A14–A15. Retrieved from: http://chronicle.com/article/Female-Veterans-Can-Be-Hard-to/133205/

Sander, L. (2013, December 20). With GI bill at milestone, veterans push for campus services. *Chronicle of Higher Education*, p. A6. Retrieved from: http://chronicle.com/article/As-GI-Bill-Reaches-Milestone/143597/

Schlossberg, N. K. (2011). Commentary. In D. DiRamio & K. Jarvis, *Veterans in higher education: When Johnny and Jane came marching to campus* (p. 18). ASHE Higher Education Report, *37*(3). Hoboken, NJ: Wiley & Sons.

Schults, J. R., Bell, K. M., Naugle, A. E. & Polusrry, M. A. (2006). Child sexual abuse and adulthood sexual assault among military veteran and civilian women. *Military Medicine*, *171*, 723–728.

143

Schwartz, S. (1986). The relative earnings of Vietnam and Korean-era veterans. *Industrial and Labor Relations Review, 20,* 564–572. Retrieved from: http://jstor.org/stable/2523248

Segal, M. W., Thanner, M. H. & Segal, D. R. (2007). Hispanic and African American women and men in the U.S. military: Trends in representation. *Race, Gender, & Class, 14*(3/4), 48–64. Retrieved from: http://www.jstor.org/stable/41675289

Service Women's Action Network (SWAN). (2014). *Military sexual violence: Rape, sexual assault, and sexual harassment.* Retrieved from: http://servicewomen.org/military-sexual-violence/

Shackelford, A. L. (2009). Documenting the needs of student veterans with disabilities: Intersection roadblocks, solutions, and legal realities. *Journal of Postsecondary Education and Disability, 22*(1), 36–42.

Shaffer, D. R. (2004). *After the glory: The struggles of Black Civil War veterans.* Lawrence, KS: University of Kansas Press.

Shanker, T. & Cooper, H. (2014, February 23). Pentagon plans to shrink Army to pre-World War II level. *The New York Times.* Retrieved from: http://www.nytimes.com/2014/02/24/us/politics/pentagon-plans-to-shrink-army-to-pre-world-war-ii-level.html?_r=0

Shatuck, N. L. & Brown, S.A.T. (2013). Wounded in action: What the sleep community can learn from sleep disorders of the US Military service members. *Sleep, 36,* 159–160. Retrieved from: http://dx.doi.org/10.5665/sleep.2356

Shea, K. P. & Fishback, S. J. (2012). Impact of cumulative combat stress on learning in an academic environment. In J. Zacharakis & C. L. Polson (Eds.), *Beyond training: The rise of adult education in the military* (New Directions for Adult and Continuing Education, No. 136, pp. 53–63). San Francisco: Jossey-Bass.

Shearer, B. F. (1979). An experiment in military and civilian education: The Students' Army Training Corps at the University of Illinois. *Journal of Illinois State Historical Society, 72,* 213–224. Retrieved from: http://www.jstor.org/stable/40191276

Shipherd, J. C., Mizock, L., Maguen, S. & Green, K. E. (2012). Male-to-female transgender veterans and VA Health Care utilization. *International Journal of Sexual Health, 24,* 78–87, doi: 10.1080/19317611.2011.639440

Simpson, A. & Armstrong, S. (2009). From the military to the civilian work force: Addressing veteran career development concerns. *Career Planning and Adult Development Journal, 25,* 177–187.

Smith, N. G. & Ingram, K. M. (2004). Workplace heterosexism and adjustment among lesbian, gay, and bisexual individuals: The role of unsupportive social interactions. *Journal of Counseling Psychology, 51,* 57–67, doi: 10.1037/0022–0167.51.1.57

Smithee, M., Greenblatt, S. L. & Eland, A. (2004). *U.S. cultural series: U.S. classroom culture.* Washington, DC: NAFSA: Association of International Educators.

Smole, D. P. & Loane, S. S. (2008, July 3). *A brief history of veterans' education benefits and their value* (Congressional Report no. RL34549). Washington, DC: Library of Congress Congressional Research Service. Retrieved from: http://assets.opencrs.com/rpts/RL34549_20080703.pdf

Sobel, S. L., Westcott, K. S., Benecke, M. M., Osburn, C. D. & Cleghorn, J. M. (2000). *Conduct unbecoming: The sixth annual report on "don't ask, don't tell, don't pursue, don't harass."* Retrieved from Servicemembers Legal Defense Network website: http://sldn.3cdn.net/bc84613306fbdcf69d_gkm6iyfnf.pdf

Sobel, S. L., Cleghorn, J. M. & Osburn, C. D. (2001). *Unbecoming: The seventh annual report on "don't ask, don't tell, don't pursue, don't harass."* Retrieved from Servicemembers Legal Defense Network website: http://sldn.3cdn.net/cb11db6afdbe882794_jbm6iidrb.pdf

Soeters, J. L. (1997). Value orientations in military academies: A thirteen country study. *Armed Forces & Society, 24,* 7–32.

Soeters, J. L., Poponete, C. & Page, J. T. (2006). Culture's consequences in the military. In T. W. Britt, A. B. Adler & C. A. Castro (Eds.), *Military life: The psychology of service in peace and combat: Vol. 4. Military Culture* (pp. 13–34). Westport, CT: Praeger.

Stake, R. E. (2005). *Multiple case-study analysis.* New York, NY: Guilford.

Stanley, M. (2003). College education and the midcentury GI Bills. *Quarterly Journal on Economics, 118,* 671–708, doi: 10.1162/003355303321675482

Street, A. E., Vogt, D. & Dutra, L. (2009). A new generation of women veterans: Stressors faced by women deployed to Iraq and Afghanistan. *Clinical Psychology Review, 29,* 685–694, doi: 10.1016/j.cpr.2009.08.0

Student Veterans of America. (2013a). *Our story: SVA's predecessors.* Retrieved from: http://studentveterans.org/about-us/history.html

Student Veterans of America. (2013b). *Tracking our student veterans' progress.* Retrieved from: http://www.gotyour6.org/tracking-our-student-veterans-progress/

Takaki, R. (2000). *Double victory: A multicultural history of America in World War II.* New York, NY: Back Bay Books.

Talburt, S. (2004). Ethnographic respponsibility without the "real." *Journal of Higher Education, 75,* 80–99.

Taylor, L. S. (1988). Invasion of the home front: The veterans at Arkansas State Teachers College, 1945–1949. *The Arkansas Historical Quarterly, 74,* 116–136. Retrieved from: http://www.jstor.org/stable/40038145

Tinto, V. (1993). *Leaving college: Rethinking the causes and cures of student attrition* (2nd ed.). Chicago, IL: University of Chicago Press.

Thelin, J. R. (2011). *A history of American higher education* (2nd ed.). Baltimore, MD: Johns Hopkins University Press.

Toporek, R. L. & Liu, W. M. (2001). Advocacy in counseling: Addressing race, class, and gender oppression. In D. B. Pope-Davis & H.L.K. Coleman (Eds.), *The intersection of race, class, and gender in multicultural counseling* (pp. 285–413). Thousand Oaks, CA: Sage.

Toporek, R. L., Lewis, J. A. & Crethar, H. C. (2009). Promoting systemic change through the ACA advocacy competencies. *Journal of Counseling & Development, 87,* 260–287.

Torres, V., Jones, S. R. & Renn, K. A. (2009). Identity development theories in student affairs: Origins, current status, and new approaches. *Journal of College Student Development*, *50*, 577–596.

Turner, S. & Bound, J. (2003). Closing the gap or welding the divide: The effects of the G.I. Bill and World War II on the educational outcomes of Black Americans. *The Journal of Economic History*, *63*, 145–177. Retrieved from: http:// www.jstor.org/stable/3132498

University of Missouri Veteran Task Force. (2008). *Report of the chancellor's task force for a veteran-friendly campus*. Unpublished manuscript. University of Missouri, Columbia, Missouri.

Uribe, M. (Interviewer) & Cano, T. (Interviewee) (2013). *University housing model could help veterans* [Interview transcript]. Retrieved from NPR website: http://www.npr.org/2013/02/19/172373137/new-university-housing-model-could-help-veterans

U.S. Census Bureau. (2012). *Profile America facts for features*. Retrieved from: http://www.census.gov/newsroom/releases/archives/facts_for_features_special_editions/cb13-ff27.html

U.S. Department of Defense. (2012). *2012 demographics profile of the military community*. Retrieved from: http://www.militaryonesource.mil/12038/MOS/Reports/2012_Demographics_Report.pdf

U.S. Department of Education. (2011, April 22). *Centers of excellence for student veteran success*. Retrieved from: http://www2.ed.gov/programs/cevss/index.html

U.S. Department of Labor. (2011). *Trauma-informed care for women veterans experiencing homelessness: A guide for service providers*. Retrieved from: http://www.dol.gov/wb/trauma/WBTraumaGuide2011.pdf

U.S. Department of Veterans Affairs. (n.d.). *VA history in brief*. Retrieved from: http://www.va.gov/opa/publications/archives/docs/history_in_brief.pdf

U.S. Department of Veterans Affairs. (1990). *Application of dual compensation to veteran-student services program* (Vet. Aff. Op. Gen. Couns. Prec. 45–90). Retrieved from: www.va.gov/ogc/opinions/1990precedentopinions.asp

U.S. Department of Veterans Affairs. (2001). *VEAP and section 903* (22–79–1). Retrieved from: http://www.benefits.va.gov/gibill/docs/pamphlets/ch32_pamphlet.pdf

U.S. Department of Veterans Affairs. (2011). *America's women veterans: Military service history and VA benefit utilization statistics*. Retrieved from: http://www.va.gov/vetdata/docs/specialreports/final_womens_report_3_2_12_v_7.pdf

U.S Department of Veterans Affairs. (2012, May). *Post 9/11 GI Bill: It's your future, Yellow Ribbon Program*. Retrieved from: http://www.benefits.va.gov/gibill/docs/pamphlets/Yellow_Ribbon_Pamphlet.pdf

U.S. Department of Veterans Affairs. (2013a, November 21). *About GI bill: History and timeline*. Retrieved from: http://www.benefits.va.gov/gibill/history.asp

U.S. Department of Veterans Affairs. (2013b). *Montgomery GI Bill*. Retrieved from: http://www.benefits.va.gov/gibill/montgomery_bill.asp

U.S. Department of Veterans Affairs. (2013c, February 8). *Providing health care for transgender and intersex veterans.* VHA DIRECTIVE 2013–003. Retrieved from: http://www.va.gov/vhapublications/ViewPublication.asp?pub_ID=2863

U.S. Department of Veterans Affairs. (2013d, November, 20). *Veterans' opportunity to work.* Retrieved from: http://www.benefits.va.gov/vow/

U.S. Department of Veterans Affairs. (2013e). *Women veteran profile.* Retrieved from: http://www.va.gov/vetdata/docs/SpecialReports/Women_Veteran_Profile5.pdf

U.S. Department of Veterans Affairs. (2014a). *Benefits.* Retrieved from: http://www.benefits.va.gov/benefits/

U.S. Department of Veterans Affairs. (2014b). *Who are today's service members?* Retrieved from: http://www.va.gov/vetsinworkplace/docs/em_todaysServiceMembers.asp

U.S. Department of Veterans Health Administration. (2013). *The military health-history pocket card for clinicians.* Retrieved from: http://www.va.gov/oaa/pocketcard/military-health-history-card-for-print.pdf

U.S. Government Accountability Office. (2011). *Veterans' education benefits: Enhanced guidance and collaboration could improve administration of the post-9/11 GI Bill program* (GAO Publication no. GAO 11–356R). Retrieved from: http://www.gao.gov/new.items/d11356r.pdf

U.S. Navy Recruiting Command. (n.d.). *Navy recruiting facts and statistics.* Retrieved from: http://www.cnrc.navy.mil/facts-and-stats.htm

Vacchi, D. T. (2012, June). Considering student veterans on the twenty-first-century college campus. *About Campus, 17,* 15–21, doi: 10.1002/abc.21075

Ward, C. (1996). Acculturation. In D. Landis & R. Bhagat (Eds.), *Handbook of intercultural training* (2nd ed., pp. 124–147). Newbury Park, CA: Sage.

Weick, K. E. (2005). Organizing and failures of imagination. *International Public Management Journal, 8,* 425–438, doi: 10.1080/10967490500439883

Welch, IV, J. (2007). The role of intuition in interdisciplinary thought. *Issues in Integrative Studies, 25,* 131–155. Retrieved from: http://www.units.miamioh.edu/aisorg/PUBS/ISSUES/25_welch.pdf

Whitley, K., Tschudi, P. E. & Giber, C. T. (2013, October). *Life beyond war: Supporting the mental health needs of student veterans.* Symposium conducted at the HSC Foundation, Washington, DC. Retrieved from: http://www.hscfoundation.org/pdf/whitepaper_veterans%20final_508.pdf

Williams, C. L. & Berry, J. W. (1991). Primary prevention of acculturative stress among refugees: Application of psychological theory and practice. *American Psychologist, 46,* 632–641, doi: 10.1037/0003-066X.46.6.632

Wilmot, M. (2013). Women warriors: From making milestones in the military to community reintegration. In R. M. Scurfield & K. T. Platino (Eds.), *War trauma and its wake: Expanding the circle of healing* (pp. 69–87). New York, NY: Routledge.

Wilson, S. (1958). G. I. In A. C. Spectorsky (Ed.), *The college years* (pp. 160–163). New York, NY: Hawthorn.

Wilson, K. & Smith, N. (2012). Understanding the importance of life mission when advising soldiers. In J. Zacharakis & C. J. Polsom (Eds.), *Beyond training: The rise of adult education in the military* (New Directions for Adult and Continuing Education, No. 136, pp. 65–75). San Francisco, CA: Jossey Bass.

Yerke, A. F. & Mitchell, V. (2013). Transgender people in the military: Don't ask? Don't tell? Don't enlist! *Journal of Homosexuality*, *60*, 436–457, doi: 10.1080/00918369.2013.744933

Yin, R. K. (2009). *Case study research: Design and methods* (4th ed.). Applied Social Research Methods Series, 5. Los Angeles, CA: Sage.

Zinger, L. & Cohen, A. (2010). Veterans returning from war into the classroom: How can colleges be better prepared to meet their needs. *Contemporary Issues in Education Research*, *3*(1), 38–51. Retrieved from: http://search.proquest.com.mutex.gmu.edu/docview/196350958?accountid=14541

Appendix

RESOURCE LIST

The list below contains websites and documentary films that may be valuable to the reader. First, we present sources of data and pending legislation regarding concerns of SVSM. Then we list sources consistent with the sections in Chapter 5, "Best Practices for Increasing Student Success." We highlight association websites that readers may find particularly useful, which include practical guides, tools, conferences, networks, and training resources for creating a multicultural campus that integrates SVSM into the college community. Last, we list websites about documentary films that present the culture and experiences of SVSM in a powerful visual format.

Data

American Fact Finder
   http://factfinder2.census.gov/faces/nav/jsf/pages/index.xhtml
Integrated Post-Secondary Education Data System
   http://nces.ed.gov/ipeds/
Retired Military Statistics by Congressional District
   http://actuary.defense.gov/
State Wide Statistics by Program Type
   http://www.vba.va.gov/REPORTS/abr/2012_abr.pdf
U.S. Department of Veterans Affairs, *Statistics on Veterans*
   http://www.va.gov/vetdata/index.asp
U.S. Department of Veterans Affairs, *Veteran Population—County Level by Age and Gender*
   http://www.va.gov/vetdata/veteran_population.asp

Legislation

Open Congress, Pending Legislations
   http://www.opencongress.org/bill/pending

The U.S. Senate, Committee on Veterans' Affairs
   http://www.veterans.senate.gov/legislation

For Higher Education Institutions

ACPA College Student Educators International
   http://www.acpa.nche.edu/

American Association of Community Colleges
   http://www.aacc.nche.edu

American Council on Education, *Military Students and Veterans*
   http://www.acenet.edu/higher-education/Pages/Military-Students-and-Veterans.aspx

American Council on Education, *Toolkit for Veteran Friendly Institutions*
   https://vetfriendlytoolkit.acenet.edu/Pages/default.aspx

Council of Colleges and Military Educators (CCME)
   http://www.ccmeonline.org/

Defense Activity for Non-Traditional Education Support
   http://www.dantes.doded.mil/educational-institutions/index.html

NASPA—Student Affairs Administrators in Higher Education
   https://www.naspa.org/

National Student Clearinghouse
   http://www.studentclearinghouse.org/

Operation College Promise
   http://www.operationpromiseforservicemembers.com/

Servicemembers Opportunity Colleges
   http://www.soc.aascu.org/

Student Veterans of America
   http://www.studentveterans.org/

U.S. Department of Veterans Services, Education and Training
   http://www.benefits.va.gov/gibill/

U.S. Department of Veterans Affairs, *Yellow Ribbon Program*
   http://www.benefits.va.gov/GIBILL/yellow_ribbon/Yellow_Ribbon_Info_Schools.asp

VA Campus Toolkit
   http://www.mentalhealth.va.gov/StudentVeteran/#sthash.2XKEGAly.dpbs

Veterans in Higher Education National Clearinghouse
http://vets.arizona.edu/clearinghouse/

Veterans Upward Bound
http://www2.ed.gov/programs/triovub/index.html

Yellow Ribbon Events
http://www.yellowribbon.mil

Campus Veterans Services

Council for the Advancement of Standards in Higher Education (2012). *CAS professional standards for higher education* (8th ed.). Washington, DC: CAS. www.cas.edu

National Association of Veterans' Program Administrators
http://www.navpa.org/

Tutor.com for U.S. Military Families (free tutoring services for SVSM)
http://www.tutor.com/military

U.S. Department of Veterans Affairs, *National Resource Directory*
https://www.ebenefits.va.gov/ebenefits/nrd

U.S. Department of Veterans Affairs, *State Veterans Affairs Offices*
http://www.va.gov/statedva.htm

U.S. Department of Veterans Affairs, *VA Facility Locator*
http://www2.va.gov/directory/guide/allstate.asp

U.S. Department of Veterans Affairs, *Workstudy*
http://www.benefits.va.gov/gibill/workstudy.asp

Veterans National Honor Society
http://salute.colostate.edu/

Counseling Centers

Center for Deployment Psychology
http://www.deploymentpsych.org/

Defense Centers for Excellence for Psychological Health and Traumatic Brain Injury
http://www.dcoe.mil/

EMDR Institute, Inc.
http://www.emdr.com/general-information/what-is-emdr.html

EMDR International Association
http://www.emdria.org/

National Alliance of Mental Illness (NAMI), *Veterans and Military Resource Center*
http://www.nami.org/Template.cfm?Section=Veterans_Resources&
Template=/ContentManagement/ContentDisplay.cfm&Content
ID=53242&lstid=877

National Suicide Prevention Lifeline
http://www.suicidepreventionlifeline.org/

PTSD: National Center for PTSD
http://www.ptsd.va.gov/

The Jed Foundation, *Helping Our Student Veterans Succeed*
https://www.jedfoundation.org/professionals/programs-and-research/
helping-our-student-veterans-succeed

Vet Center Program
http://www.vetcenter.va.gov/

Veterans Crisis Line
http://www.veteranscrisisline.net/

U.S. Department of Veterans Affair, *Mental Health Provider Training*
http://www.mentalhealth.va.gov/index.asp

Enrollment Management

American Association of Collegiate Registrars and Admissions Officers
http://www.aacrao.org/

American Council on Education, *College Credit for Military Services*
http://www.acenet.edu/higher-education/topics/Pages/College-Credit-
for-Military-Service.aspx

American Council on Education, *Military Evaluations*
http://www.acenet.edu/higher-education/topics/Pages/Military-
Evaluations.aspx

American Council on Education, *Toolkit for Veteran Friendly Institutions, Admissions
and Financial Aid*
https://vetfriendlytoolkit.acenet.edu/admissions-and-financial-aid/
Pages/default.aspx

Health Centers

American Medical Association, *Supporting Veterans Health*
http://www.ama-assn.org/ama/pub/physician-resources/public-health/
joining-forces.page

Deployment Health Clinical Center
http://www.pdhealth.mil/

Mild Traumatic Brain Injury—Concussion, Pocket Guide for Clinicians
http://www.publichealth.va.gov/docs/exposures/TBI-pocketcard.pdf

U.S. Department of Veterans Affairs, *Military Health History Pocket Card for Clinicians*
http://www.va.gov/oaa/pocketcard/Military-Health-History-Card-for-print.pdf

Disability Services

American Council on Education, *Accommodating student veterans with traumatic brain injury and posttraumatic stress disorder: Tips for campus faculty and staff*
http://www.acenet.edu/news-room/Documents/Accommodating-Student-Veterans-with-Traumatic-Brain-Injury-and-Post-Traumatic-Stress-Disorder.pdf

Association on Higher Education and Disability (AHEAD), *Veterans with Disabilities in Higher Education*
http://www.ahead.org/SIGs/veterans

Disabled American Veterans
http://www.dav.org/

The Defense and Veterans Brain Injury Center (DVBIC), *Back to school: Guide to academic success after traumatic brain injury*
http://dvbic.dcoe.mil/sites/default/files/Back%20to%20School%20Academic%20Success%20After%20TBI.pdf

The University of Arizona, Disabled Veterans Reintegration and Education Project (DVRE)
http://drc.arizona.edu/veterans-reintegration-education/

U.S. Department of Veterans Affairs, *Vocational rehabilitation and employment*
http://www.benefits.va.gov/vocrehab/links_resources.asp

Career Services

American Corporate Partners (ACP)
http://www.acp-usa.org/

Career One Stop
http://www.careeronestop.org/ReEmployment/Veterans/Default.aspx

Computer/Electronics Accommodations Program
http://cap.mil/Programs/WSM/WSMAdditionalResources.aspx

National Career Development Association (NCDA), *Veterans' Task Force—Research Committee, bibliography of military career transition research 2000–present*
  http://www.ncda.org/aws/NCDA/asset_manager/get_file/65078

U.S. Department of Veterans Affairs, *The VetSuccess on campus*
  https://www.vetsuccess.va.gov/public/vetsuccess_on_campus.html

U.S. Department of Veterans Affairs, *Transition Assistance Program (TAP)*
  http://www.benefits.va.gov/VOW/tap.asp

U.S. Department of Labor, *Veterans' Employment and Training Services (VETS)*
  http://www.dol.gov/vets/

U.S. Department of Veterans Affairs, *Vet Success Program*
  https://www.vetsuccess.va.gov/public/index.html?PHPSESSID=bc064b2fbff5c84d7d8ee0d7b5c84986

U.S. Department of Veterans Affairs, *Vocational rehabilitation and employment*
  http://www.benefits.va.gov/vocrehab/links_resources.asp

Academic Advising

National Academic Advising Association (NACADA), *Advising veterans resource links*
  http://www.nacada.ksu.edu/Resources/Clearinghouse/View-Articles/Advising-veterans-resource-links.aspx

Multicultural Student Affairs

Black Veterans for Social Justice
  http://www.bvsj.org/

National Association for Black Veterans (NABVETS)
  http://www.nabvets.org/

Native American Veterans Association
  http://www.navavets.com/

The Society of Hispanic Veterans
  http://hispanicveterans.org/

United Mexican-American Veterans Association (UMAVA)
  http://umava.org/

Women's Centers

American Women Veterans
  http://americanwomenveterans.org/home/

Business and Professional Women's Foundation (BPW), Joining Forces for
Women Veterans' Mentorship Program
http://bpwfoundation.org/index.php/issues/women_veterans

U.S. Department of Veterans Affairs, *Center for Woman Veterans*
http://www1.va.gov/womenvet/

National Women Veterans of America
http://www.wvanational.org/

Gay, Lesbian, Bisexual, & Transgender (GLBT) Resource Centers

American Veterans for Equal Rights (AVER)
http://aver.us/

OutServe-Servicemembers Legal Defense Network (SLDN)
http://www.sldn.org/

The American Military Partner Association (AMPA)
http://militarypartners.org/

The Palm Center
http://www.palmcenter.org/

Transgender American Veterans Association (TAVA)
http://tavausa.org/

Documentary Films

Crisis Hotline: Veterans Press 1
http://www.hbo.com/documentaries/crisis-hotline-veterans-press-1#/

Free the Mind: Can You Rewire the Brain Just by Taking a Breath?
http://danishdocumentary.com/site/freethemind/

Ground Operation: Battlefields to Farmfields
http://www.groundoperations.net/

Invisible Wounds—Break Down
http://m.youtube.com/watch?v=vBX-1pAyXnI

The Invisible War
http://invisiblewarmovie.com/watch.php

Lioness
http://www.lionessthefilm.com/

"Now and After"(PTSD from Soldier's POV)
http://m.youtube.com/watch?v=NkWwZ9ZtPEI

155

Restrepo
    http://movies.nationalgeographic.com/movies/restrepo/

Service: When Women Come Marching Home
    http://servicethefilm.com/index.php

The Invisible Ones: Homeless Combat Veterans
    http://www.theinvisibleones.org/index.html

Veterans Documentary Corps
    http://veterandocs.org/

Warriors Return
    http://servicethefilm.com/warriorsreturn/

Wartorn
    http://m.youtube.com/watch?v=5miBVm3B6tM

Where Soldiers Come From
    http://www.wheresoldierscomefrom.com/

Index

References to figures are shown in *italics*. References to tables are shown in **bold**.

159

161